Collectible

Souvenir Spoons

Identification

& Values

By

Wayne
Bednersh

COLLECTOR BOOKS

A Division of Schroeder Publishing Co., Inc.

Searching For A Publisher?

We are always looking for knowledgeable people considered to be experts within their fields. If you feel that there is a real need for a book on your collectible subject and have a large comprehensive collection, contact Collector Books.

Cover Design by Terri Stalions
Book Design by Karen Smith

Collector Books
P.O. Box 3009
Paducah, Kentucky 42002-3009

Printed in the U.S.A. by Image Graphics, Paducah, KY

Contents

Acknowledgments

I would like to thank the following people for the very extensive help they rendered in letting me photograph portions of their collections and giving me significant guidance and much historical information. Without their significant help and encouragement, this volume could not have been produced: Lynn Randall, Diane Zinn, Alamae Pierce, Carol Hyland, Bob Corson, and Constance Halket.

I would also like to thank the librarians and researchers of the Los Angeles Public Library, in particular at the Woodland Hills branch, for their significant help in doing needed research: Michael Eisenberg, Woodland Hills Library; Marie Bougetz.

I would like to thank the following people for helping me in the initial process of learning how to write interesting articles about spoons and silver: Dorothy Rainwater, author of many books about spoons and silver; Connie McNally, publisher of *Silver Magazine*; Diane Zinn, author of many articles about spoons.

I would also like to thank the members of the Spoon Collectors of Southern California for significant support and guidance during the production of this book.

I would further like to thank Dennis Entin for superb help above and beyond the call of duty for keeping my computer running under trying circumstances. During the course of writing this volume I had to replace one computer system and required a number of software adjustments to make the system useful.

Finally, but definitely not last, I would like to thank my wife, Cherilyn Bednersh, for her support and encouragement.

Introduction to Spoons

It is almost impossible to write a book which will appeal equally to very advanced collectors and novices as well as those who just need a quick reference source. Yet that is what I have attempted to do.

For the advanced collector, I have tried to show a number of rarer spoons, yet I have not written in depth about any particular spoon as previous authors have done. Instead, at the editor's urging, I have chosen to show a much wider variety of spoons and more pictures than any other American spoon book ever published. In many cases, I have chosen to show only portions of the spoon so that the incredible details can be more easily seen. If more specific research is needed for a particular spoon, the usual sources of the library and encyclopedia are recommended.

For the intermediate collector, the wide variety of spoons shown will help you choose a specialization area and will give a broader variety of examples than you have seen in any other single source. I hope this book will give you greater insight into the fantastic world of spoon collecting.

For the novice collector and for dealers, this book will serve as a reference and a guide for the buying and selling of American spoons (please read the section on prices). It is estimated that there are over 50,000 different varieties of American spoons, thus it is simply not possible to show each one. But by comparing your spoons to the pieces shown, you will have a much better feeling for the entire spoon world.

The most important part of this book for all readers is to simply enjoy the pictures. Yes, the spoons are beautiful; yes, they are important American antiques; yes, they are valuable, but in the final analysis, they should simply be *enjoyed*.

Pricing Information

Prices

Price ranges are provided for most of the spoons shown. The price for any collectible is based upon supply and demand. Souvenir spoons are not an exception. There are an estimated 50,000 different spoon variations and it is not possible to give exact prices for each variation. In addition the price for the same spoon will vary quite widely depending on the geographic region and the type of sales venue. Since souvenir spoons are sold at widely different venues ranging from garage sales, flea markets, antique stores, auctions, and upscale antique shows, it is not surprising that we find a tremendous range of prices. Furthermore some subject matters will be of no interest to a dealer, but might be of significant interest to a particular collector; thus we find price ranges of several hundred percent for the same spoon. In addition, a different bowl on the same handle or vice versa may materially affect the price of a spoon. A plain bowl or one with just initials, a place location, or date is not worth as much as a nicely designed picture bowl. Of major importance is the dealer. Knowledgeable informed dealers will price most pieces at a fair market price based upon their costs to acquire the item, selling expenses, and required profit margins. A dealer who is selling in a parking lot will not be able to obtain the top prices as would a dealer in a posh showroom or at an open auction. Uninformed dealers will normally price items at unrealistic levels (either too high or too low). The purpose of the price ranges is to give both dealers and customers realistic expectations. The price ranges are NOT absolutes and change frequently. They should be used only as guidelines. Many will be invalid before this volume is printed. Dealers must remember that without customers they will not be in business, and customers must remember that without dealers, they will not have an opportunity to acquire new items.

Condition

Obviously condition is important, but most souvenir spoons were designed to be display pieces, thus very few of them have seen substantial use. There is no grading system similar to those that exist for some types of collectibles such as coins or prints. Therefore unless a piece shows visible damage, condition is not a major factor.

Enameled and plique-à-jour pieces, however, chip very easily and must be examined very carefully because any damage will severely impact the price. For plique-à-jour, hold the piece up to the light and examine it very carefully. It is very difficult and expensive to have repaired. It is usually possible to see where enamel is chipped if examined carefully. When the enamel is applied in fine lines, it also tends to chip very easily. Enamel repairs can sometimes be made, but it is often difficult to get the color to match exactly and the repairs may be expensive. The price of these spoons will decline very substantially if they are damaged.

Sterling silver will tarnish when exposed to air. Unless the tarnish is so excessive that the piece has turned black, tarnish does not materially affect the price since it is usually easily cleaned by standard silver cleaning polishes. Dealers should avoid the use of "instant" cleaners which tend to give the spoon a very unnatural look that could lower the price. Dealers, if you have a tarnished piece in stock and it was clean when you first tried to sell it, the price is too high!

Copper, aluminum, stainless steel, and silver-plated spoons normally sell for significantly less than sterling spoons. But simply because a spoon is sterling silver does not mean it will command a high price. When these spoons were made, the value of the silver to the selling price was substantial. The value of silver as a percentage of the selling price is now much lower. The typical spoon has between ½ and ¾ of an ounce of silver; the value of that silver is now less than $4.00. Artistic quality and other factors are much more important.

Rarity

Rarity in souvenir spoons is very hard to assess. Obviously some pieces are readily available, and some pieces are seldom seen. But even experts who have seen hundreds of thousands of spoons cannot remember all of the variations. The great majority of souvenir spoons could be classified as relatively rare by most collectible standards as most examples were created in relatively small quantities, unlike stamps or coins which may have had mintage in the hundreds of thousands. Even common spoons were often created in production runs of under 3,000. In addition, many spoons have been lost, melted, damaged or destroyed over the years.

We can classify spoons in common categories, however. For example, there is a chapter which discusses high school spoons. It is very common for a collector or dealer to encounter such pieces, but there are so many different high schools pictured that each one is rare. If a dealer were to price a high school spoon based upon its relative rarity, it would remain in stock for a very long time, unless the dealer were to get lucky and find someone interested in that particular school. It would be much more logical to price the item reasonably and thus make a faster sale. A famous retailer said, "It is better to make a fast nickel than a slow dime."

Beauty and Subject Matter

Of most importance to most spoon collectors is the beauty and subject matter (i.e., it fits with their specialty). Since beauty is definitely in the eye of the beholder, dealers should not make unwarranted assumptions unless they have significant experience dealing with spoons. Many a novice dealer will see a complex state seal design, for example, and assume that it is extremely valuable which is simply not true. Most spooners (spoon collectors) have decided to specialize since it would be prohibitively expensive to make a meaningful collection of all types of spoons. Most collectors will thus make a buy or no-buy decision based upon how well the piece fits their collection and price. Since most spoon collectors will also acquire pieces outside their specialty, dealers can influence the buying decision based upon pricing.

Size

Manufactured souvenir spoons were generally made in three sizes, large teaspoon, smaller teaspoon (5 o'clock), and demitasse (demi or coffee). Some popular designs were made in all three sizes, while most spoons were only made in one size. The larger, heavier spoons are generally more valuable than the smaller spoons. Demi spoons are usually very lightweight and sell for less. A very high percentage of demi spoons is also available in the larger sizes. Of course size is just one of many factors.

Value

Souvenir spoons were relatively expensive souvenirs and were marketed to upscale families. The typical spoon wholesaled between one and three dollars and retailed for even more. That doesn't sound like a lot of money, until we factor in the concept of inflation. Around the turn of the century, the average skilled working man made 25 cents an hour. Many made substantially less, and 5 or 10 cents an hour jobs were fairly common. We must also remember that the average job was 10–12 hours per day and most

people worked six days a week. A skilled working man would have to work 16 to 20 hours to buy a typical souvenir spoon. Supposing that a typical skilled workman today is making $12 per hour, the equivalent value of that spoon would be ($12/hour times 16–20 hours of work) or $192 – $240. Since it is obvious that most of the spoons today sell for substantially less than that, we can only conclude that the value of these spoons has not kept pace with labor inflation.

Furthermore in inflation-adjusted dollars, sterling souvenir spoons are one of the least expensive quality Victorian era antiques available to today's collectors. Not only can the collector buy these beautiful detailed silver antiques (most are between 80 and 110 years old) at relatively cheap "pre-inflation" prices, but they are also acquiring and preserving important artifacts of our country's culture. In addition, many of the skills required to make these spoons, such as picture engraving and plique-à-jour work, are no longer available to industry, so it is unlikely that we will see items of this quality available in the future.

Manufacturers

For the most part, souvenir spoon collectors are not overly concerned with which firm manufactured a particular spoon and a number of rarer specimens are not marked. Spoons without a manufacturer marking do not sell for significantly less than an equivalent piece with the marking. Both Tiffany and Gorham were considered the top silver manufacturers at the time. Gorham entered the souvenir business with gusto and produced a number of fine designs in quantity. These spoons now sell for prices equivalent to any other manufacturer. Tiffany produced only a few souvenir spoon designs in very limited quantities. These spoons sell at a premium of about 10–25 percent more than an equivalent spoon from another manufacturer. This is probably due more to the prominence of the Tiffany name in other collectible areas and relative rarity rather than to superior design.

Reproductions

The late Victorian era saw a large number of reproductions of older spoons. Some of these copied the older pieces' styling and used legitimate markings. Some of them copied the older pieces and used marks that were deliberately designed to confuse. Most of these situations occurred with European pieces and thus are not a major concern with American spoons. Simply look for the word "sterling" on most American spoons. In most cases of

American spoons the absence of the word "sterling" or "925" will imply that the item is silver plated and probably not a desirable collectible. There are exceptions, but it takes considerable skill to recognize them.

It was quite common for one manufacturer to copy an existing successful design of another manufacturer and make only very minor changes. Lawsuits filed in court attest to this practice, plus we often see pieces that are so similar we would guess that they were from the same die molds. Generally speaking, it is difficult to know which was the original and there is usually not a price difference.

In a number of cases, the dies for some American souvenir spoons were acquired by other companies by purchase of the dies or outright purchase or merger of the company and the spoons were "re-issued." Most of these re-issues were contemporaneous and thus are treated the same as the originals. The only difference may be the manufacturer mark on the back of the piece. There is usually no price difference.

In a few cases, spoons were re-issues but were silverplated and usually readily recognized. But sometimes they are so well done that an acid test has to be performed. Your author even bought one of these recently. Generally speaking they do not represent a significant problem. A few spoons have been later copied by electroform, but these were so poorly done that again a major problem has not occurred. In a few cases, early spoons have been re-issued by a quality manufacturer. I have identified some of these in the text, but no guarantees are issued to indicate that all such re-issues have been identified.

For the vast majority of cases, the buyer of American sterling souvenir spoons is acquiring exactly what he or she expects: a high quality sterling silver antique which celebrates an important facet of our culture. As a collector, you do not have to worry about fakes or frauds unless you are specializing in expensive pieces. Collectors who specialize in such expensive antiques should also realize that the dies for many spoons still exist and they could be put into production very easily. The machinery and the knowledge to reproduce these pieces still exist at most silver manufacturers. Unless the new spoons were marked in some way, there would be no practical method of determining which ones were originals.

Initials

Quite often we find engraved names, initials, and dates on souvenir spoons. With sterling flatware, initials usually lower the value of the piece, but a poll taken of souvenir spoon collectors concluded that most collectors enjoy the additional bits of engraving. Only a few collectors objected but also indicated they would still buy a spoon if the additional engraving did not distract from the basic design. We can therefore conclude that initials and names will not affect the value of the spoons unless they are very obtrusive.

Gold Washed Bowls

Any spoon may have a gold washed bowl, a common option offered by manufacturers usually for about 25 cents per bowl. If used properly, the gold washing significantly enhances the total look of the bowl. If used poorly, it may actually detract from the look of the spoon. Generally speaking gold washing does not significantly affect the price of a spoon. Some spoons have highlighted gold decorations (partial gilt). This was a relatively new process and more expensive. It generally makes a prettier spoon but has only a limited effect on price.

Modern Tourist Spoons

A number of cheaply made souvenir spoons are found in virtually every tourist shop today. Very few serious collectors collect these pieces and thus they are not included in this volume. It is possible that at some future date, they will become serious collectibles. If you enjoy the interesting designs found on these pieces, they can usually be acquired in the $1 – $6 dollar range.

Non-American Spoons

Very innovative and beautiful spoons have been created in virtually every country around the world. The author and most serious spoon collectors have acquired many beautiful pieces that easily compare in quality with the American spoons. Other books have been written about these spoons and the reader should refer to those books. The collecting of non-American spoons is satisfying but more complicated and should be avoided until the collector understands more about silver, fakes, and frauds.

Early American Spoons

American silversmiths have been making silver spoons since shortly after the settlement of this country. The vast majority were made to be used and were of simpler styles. Some collectors enjoy these types of spoons and many can be readily found at reasonable prices, considering their age. After the Civil War, silversmiths became more adventurous in the design of silver flatware and during the "gilded age," many extremely interesting and innovative types of flatware were made. These do tend to be more expensive and are outside the sphere of this volume.

Non-Spoon Souvenir Flatware

Manufacturers would sometimes make souvenir forks, tongs, letter openers, sugar shells, spoon pins, etc. A few of these types of pieces have been illustrated. Not as many people tend to collect these types of pieces, but their inclusion is simply to show dealers and collectors examples of similar collectibles.

Catalog Inserts

All the catalog pages reproduced in this volume are from an undated Watson & Newell Co. catalog entitled "Souvenirs in Sterling Silver." It is believed that this catalog was published between 1900 and 1910. The prices are wholesale prices to jewelers and the spoons are priced by the dozen. Sterling souvenir spoons at wholesale were typically priced according to the weight and manufacturing costs rather than artistic value. Pricing new silver by weight is an old practice and was used by all manufacturers including the most prestigious such as Tiffany and Gorham. The prices of spoons on the collectible market are based upon other factors thus bearing no relationship to the original wholesale prices or weight.

Details – Details – Details

Artwork

Souvenir spoons are loaded with many details. Besides the exquisite artwork, every element of the spoon often has a documented history and historical reference. This volume does not delve into the history of most of these items as it is felt that most readers would find it unnecessarily encyclopedic. But a little research on any given spoon will often reveal a series of interesting historical tidbits. The reader is encouraged to consult encyclopedias, travel guides, and other historical reference materials to discover the interesting stories behind each spoon.

All the spoons shown are "sterling silver" quality, unless otherwise noted.

Usually only the front of the spoon is shown, but many spoons also have pictures on the back. Only in rare cases are both the front and back of a spoon shown.

Because most details on spoons are small, the reader will find that many partial detail photographs are presented. If the whole spoon were to be shown, the picture would have to be considerably enlarged so that all the minute details could be reproduced, and this would severely restrict the number of photographs. Therefore, in an attempt to present as comprehensive and interesting a book as possible, we have chosen to use many detailed pictures showing just the relevant parts of the spoons. This editorial decision means that many beautiful handles or bowls are not pictured.

It is not unusual to find spoons which concern more than one subject or activity. An advertising spoon which also showed a California mission could be pictured under either advertising or historical buildings. A California mission spoon could be pictured under either historical buildings or religion. Editorial decisions were made in categorizing the spoons presented.

Photography

Anyone who has tried to photograph silver will attest to the fact that it is extremely difficult to do credibly. Polished silver will reflect almost 90% of the light reaching its surface, thus it is like taking a picture in a mirror, which often results in unwanted reflections.

The spoon bowl presents a number of distinctly more complicated problems. Because of the concave shape of the bowl, light is reflected in myriad directions. Furthermore, not all spoon bowls are the same. Some are narrower and deeper while others are wider and more shallow. In addition, the way the handle is attached to the bowl will result in a number of different angles. The incredible detail in the bowl is easily skewed if the bowl is not perfectly aligned; sometimes buildings will appear to be skewed in certain directions. In most cases, this is the result of the photographic angle rather than of the actual spoon.

Photographs of plique-à-jour are also more complicated. In addition to all of the previous problems, to achieve the proper effect of a stained glass window it is necessary to have a strong light from behind the piece as well as frontal lighting.

Most of the photographs were made by the author who is not a professional photographer. Natural light was used as often as possible and a light tent was constructed to reduce unwanted reflections. The use of artificial light creates a whole new set of problems.

Despite considerable efforts and retaking of photographs, some spoons persist in showing shadows and those photographs are not as high a quality as hoped. Many of the deepest parts of the spoon bowls show a small black spot or other black lines. This is a reflection of the camera itself or the supporting apparatus. Such reflections are common in photographs of silver objects.

For the most part, the photographs are of high quality and present the spoons in a fair and consistent manner. The size of an object in a photograph is easily manipulated by the photographer, layout artist, and printer and it is possible that some photographs could be misleading in that regard.

Constance Halket and Bob Corson are also thanked for their contributions of some very good photographs.

The History of Spoons

The souvenir spoon movement is popularly traced to the advent of the Salem Witch spoons designed by Daniel Low. In 1891, George B. James Jr. compiled a catalog of souvenir spoons. In his introduction he said:

"About eighteen months ago Mr. Daniel Low, of Salem, to whom is given the credit of introducing souvenir spoons in this country, made a trip to Europe, where he brought home some beautiful examples from European silversmiths. Conceiving the idea of producing a spoon which would embody the traditions and legends of Salem, he had a die made for the Salem "Witch" Spoon. This spoon had an immense sale; others were produced, until it is now estimated that there are fully two thousand two hundred souvenir spoons in this country. Some of these spoons are exceedingly beautiful, the best efforts of the silversmiths being expended on their production; while many of them are commemorative of places and events, there are a number which are appropriate souvenirs of individuals...Many a legend which has long been forgotten in the town of its origin, many a beautiful story which has long since been lost, have been happily brought to mind, and tradition honored by its incorporation in the souvenir spoon."

It is amazing to learn that 2,200 different designs were made in the first 18 months of the souvenir spoon movement which then continued through good times and bad (surviving two major financial panics and two wars) for the next 20 years. Within the United States, numerous silversmiths and silver manufacturers participated and produced extensive lines of different and unusual spoons, but this phenomenon was a world-wide event. Souvenir spoons can be found from virtually every country on every continent, but the American spoons are the most varied, unusual, and interesting. While the bulk of the collectible spoons were created between 1891 and 1915, new spoon designs have been introduced periodically since that time. A short revival in the 1920s produced a number of interesting pointed edge Art Deco variations. At the current time, the Nordic countries are still producing a number of new and innovative designs in enameled commemorative silver spoons. Of course, non-silver and silver-plated spoons in a variety of interesting designs are still available in virtually every souvenir shop around the world.

The *Jewelers Circular* published a compilation of souvenir spoons in 1891. They asked themselves the same questions that we ask today:

"When the thinking man appreciates that the collecting of individual spoons as souvenirs of visits to certain cities and places has become a broad fashion the first question he asks within himself is, Why

should a spoon be chosen in preference to all other articles? There is no positive answer to this question; the commercial reason that a spoon admits of a combination of beauty of design and utility, and is not costly, may sustain the demand, but the demand must first be created. The very love of the spoon, which is innate in all hearts, may account for the selection. The desire for its possession is the unconscious production of a healthy mind. As all civilized people unconsciously live in accordance to a code of philosophy instituted several centuries ago, so may the demand for an article such as a spoon, in preference to another article, be the unconscious desire evolved through centuries of innate love for it."

The concept of using spoons to define one's life actually has a long history. A few examples of ancient Egyptian spoons are to be found in several museums. During the 1800s new discoveries of silver Roman spoons stirred considerable interest in the history of spoons.

In England and on the European continent, spoons with apostle finials have been known for about 500 years. These were often given to infants as baptism presents. The phrase "to be born with a silver spoon" stems from this tradition. In England examples of spoons with political motifs are known and sometimes caddy spoons were known to be used as commemoratives or souvenirs.

In the United States, examples of decorative silver spoons abound. Since a large percentage of the inhabitants of this country came from various European countries, it can be inferred that they brought their traditions with them. A few examples of American birth, marriage, and death spoons have been found, but most of these are in museums. During the post Civil War era and the "gilded age," American silversmiths were very creative and a number of fine examples of intricate silverware designs can still be found by the average collector. It is not the scope of this book to examine these patterns in detail because they are not properly considered to be souvenir spoons.

The history of the spoon is very interesting. Readers who have a deeper interest in spoon history are advised to see the books listed in the bibliography.

A Sterling Tradition

Silver Concepts

Silver was one of the metals first worked by mankind and is universally considered to be one of the two most precious metals. Gold has a high, lustrous yellow quality that the ancients attributed to the sun, and silver has a bright luminescent color which ancients attributed to the moon. Both silver and gold are relatively rare, but silver is much less rare that gold.

Silver is a relatively soft metal that can achieve an almost 90% reflectance of light creating a mirror-like shine, and it can also be easily worked with simple hand tools. By the skillful use of hammers, chisels, gravers, and tongs, it can be made into any useful shape. For thousands of years, highly skilled silversmiths have exploited these qualities and have produced some awesome examples of exquisite workmanship.

One of silver's drawbacks, however, is that in its pure state, 999 fine (999/1000), it is too soft to be used in products that are handled on a regular basis. Thousands of years ago, it was discovered that if a small percentage of copper were added to the silver, the new alloy retained the best aspects of the pure metal, but it would be much harder and thus more useful in normal life. Various percentages of copper have been used over the years to obtain these benefits.

The most common standard for the dilution of silver is Sterling, 925/1000 parts silver and 75/1000 parts copper. This standard has been used in England since the 1500s except during a brief period when the Brittania standard of 950/1000 was used. The United States officially adopted the sterling standard in the late nineteenth century although American silversmiths have used a similar quality for centuries.

The continental Europeans have typically used a 900/1000 (first quality) or an 800/1000 (second quality) standard (90% or 80%), but some parts of Europe have also used an 830/1000 or 815/1000 standard. The Russians have used a Zolotnick system which ranges between the sterling standard and the Britannia standard. Other countries have used different standards which were usually influenced by the European country with which they were closely associated.

You should not assume that sterling is the only good standard as each standard has its benefits. For example, if an item is to be subject to much use, a lower percentage of silver will yield a longer lasting product than will sterling. If the creation of the item is simply as a form of storing wealth with the intention of remelting it when financial circumstances change, then a higher percentage of silver is more important. It is only because of custom and lack of knowledge that most people believe that the only "good" standard is sterling.

On most American silver (produced after 1880), if the word "Sterling" is not on the piece, you can assume the item is not basically silver. There are a few exceptions, but it is not the province of this book to discuss those. The English use a left-facing lion to indicate sterling quality. Many other countries marked their silver in decimals to indicate the percentage of silver, e.g., .925 is equal to 925/1000 or the sterling standard. There are many other ways to mark silver objects and a number of books detail these markings.

All of the spoons which are shown in this volume are of the sterling quality unless otherwise noted, mostly because they were made in the United States after the adoption of the sterling standard and silver was less costly during this time period. American spoons are usually marked on the back by the word "Sterling" or "925." If they are marked with other designations, such as but not limited to: sp, epns, a1, Brazil silver, German silver, Colorado silver, Nevada silver, Alaska silver, albata, white silver, German silver, alpaca, aluminum silver, sterling plate, argentine, britannia, electrum, ep, epc, epbm; or if the quality is not marked, they are most likely not sterling quality and most likely not substantially

made of silver. Many of those terms are simply designed to fool the consumer because silver is relatively expensive compared to most metals and some people will try to make money by fraudulent means. The existence of this type of fraud was a basic reason that England and other countries developed their hallmarking system. Many other countries have also set standards to prevent fraud, but some fraud still exists and it is always a case of *caveat emptor* (buyer beware).

Silver plate is not silver. With silver plating a base metal, usually a zinc alloy, is covered with a very thin layer of pure silver (measured in microns). Currently an electro-chemical reaction is the preferred method used to plate base metals, but other methods of plating have also been used. With machines and mass production it is much easier and cheaper to create silver-plated flatware than it is to create a quality sterling silver product. This cheaper merchandise looks good when new, but it will not stand the test of time. However, because it is so much cheaper, many people are willing to settle for a cheaper lookalike product.

Stainless steel is not silver — it is steel. Steel is a strong building material and it can be used in flatware or other small objects. It costs less than one cent per ounce. People sometimes mix up the terms because they all start with the letter "s."

The consumer can purchase small vials of acid which when applied to an object will change color if the metal is not silver or gold. This "acid test" has been used for over a thousand years and is still the best, cheapest, and fastest way to determine if an object is really made of silver.

For the most part, the buyer of American souvenir spoons which are marked "Sterling" is getting exactly what they expect, a high quality sterling silver spoon. I have seen only a very few spoons which were marked "sterling" and turned out otherwise. Some of those were obviously copper, and the manufacurer had simply used the sterling die to create these spoons. They may have been test spoons or they may have been later restrikes.

Lady Liberty

Not like the brazen giant of Greek fame,
With conquering limbs astride from land to land;
Here at our sea-washed, sunset gates shall stand
A mighty woman with a torch, whose flame
Is the imprisoned lightning, and her name
Mother of Exiles. From her beacon-hand
Glows world-wide welcome, her mild eyes command
The air-bridged harbor that twin-cities frame
"Keep, ancient lands, your storied pomp!" cries she
With silent lips. "Give me your tired, your poor,
Your huddled masses yearning to breathe free,
The wretched refuse of your teeming shore,
Send these, the homeless, tempest-tost to me;
I lift my lamp beside the golden door!"

Emma Lazarus sonnet
inscribed on the Statue of Liberty

Plate 1

Now come with me through that golden door as we journey from coast to coast and visit a wonderous world filled with beautiful silver spoons, each bearing mute testimony to the people and grandeur of their new land.

My great-grandparents and about 15,000,000 other immigrants answered Lady Liberty's call and came to the golden land during the heyday of the great spoon movement (1891 – 1915). These brave souls risked life and limb to cross a large ocean and begin life anew in a strange culture with a different language. Most came with only the clothes on their backs and their skills and dreams in their heads. Some of them worked in the large silver factories for a pittance to make these fantastic artistic spoons. In particular, we salute the excellent quality workmanship of the silver workers. Most of the wonderful engravings and bowl paintings that are shown throughout this book are the works of the highly skilled immigrants, engravers and painters who were forced by necessity to accept low wages to earn a living. In the process, they all made their contribution and helped build a strong and mighty nation.

Plate 1: Left to right: Tiffany, $30.00 – 80.00; Shepard, $30.00 – 50.00, Gorham, $30.00 – 45.00.

Plate 2: Unmarked manufacturer, custom elk finial and twist handle with engraved bowl; $40.00 – 60.00.

Plate 2

Plate 3: Gorham; cast bowl, $50.00 – 75.00.

Plate 4: Left to right: Shiebler, demi, $30.00 – 45.00; Watson, $60.00 – 85.00; Shiebler, $80.00 – 100.00.

Plate 5: Demi Statue of Liberty; mark not traced, $20.00 – 30.00.

Plate 6: Detail bowl, $30.00 – 50.00 (tea size). Verse on spoon reads: "Thus was Manhattan again, left in primeval solitude, waiting for commerce, to come and claim its own."

Plate 3

Plate 4

Plate 5

Plate 6

Inspiring a Nation

Around the turn of the century, the mark of a well-educated person was a deep understanding of and respect for history. The United States was a young country as compared to the long-established European countries, but in its short history there were a number of people who had changed the course of its history as well as influencing that of world history. In this chapter we look at spoons commemorating explorers, founding fathers, and generals. In addition we consider some fictional characters which have historical importance.

— Explorers —

Plate 7: Stuyvesant figural with beautiful painted enamel bowl; Shepard; $150.00 – 250.00.

Plate 8: Ponce de Leon, "search for fountain of youth;" St. Augustine, Florida; no manuf. mark; $100.00 – 175.00.

Plate 9: Detroit; Dominick & Haff; $30.00 – 50.00.

Plate 10: Columbus; Coddington; $30.00 – 50.00. (See Columbian Exposition)

Plate 7

Plate 8

Plate 9

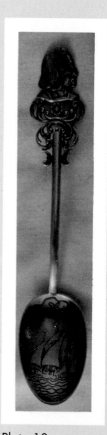

Plate 10

Plate 11: Daniel Boone, (early wilderness explorer); tobacco leaf; Gorham; round cast bowl; $85.00 – 115.00.

Plate 12: Henry Hudson, (English explorer searching for a northern route); Mechanics; $30.00 – 50.00.

Plate 13: Samuel de Champlain, (French explorer); no manuf. mark; $30.00 – 60.00.

Plate 14: Father Junipero Serra, (founder of the California missions); Watson; $50.00 – 80.00.

Plate 15: Zebulon Pike, (Western explorer); $30.00 – 60.00.

Plate 11

Plate 12

Plate 13

Plate 14

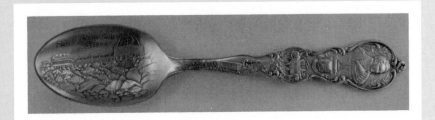

Plate 15

Plate 16: Dr. Namsen, (North Pole explorer); $50.00 – 75.00.

Plate 16

— Political Figures —

M.W. Galt Brothers produced a series of George Washington spoons around 1890. These could be called souvenir spoons, but they preceded the famous Witch spoons which are credited with starting the great souvenir spoon movement.

Plate 17 & 18: Galt Washington Spoons; $25.00 – 75.00 each.

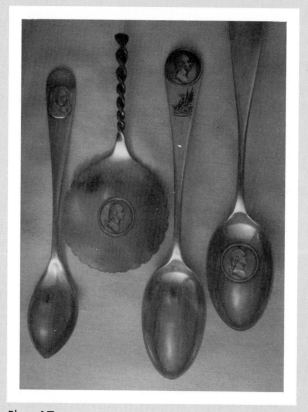

Plate 17

Plate 18

Plate 19: Washington full figural; engraved Spokane Falls bowl; Shepard; $75.00 – 125.00.

Plate 20: Washington figural; no manuf. mark; later remake; $40.00 – 85.00.

Plate 21: Washington, Valley Forge Bowl; Shiebler; $40.00 – 75.00.

Plate 22: Benjamin Franklin figural; plain bowl; no manuf. mark; $50.00 – 75.00.

Plate 23: Patrick Henry, "Give me Liberty or give me Death;" Mechanics; $40.00 – 60.00.

Plate 19

Plate 20

Plate 21

Plate 22

Plate 23

Plate 24: Andrew Jackson, (President); Gorham; $50.00 – 75.00.

Plate 25: Betsy Ross, (first American flag); Durgin; $30.00 – 50.00.

Plate 26: Abraham Lincoln, Gorham; $40.00 – 55.00.

Plate 27: Abraham Lincoln, Shiebler; $30.00 – 50.00.

Plate 28: Frederick Douglass, (famous ex-slave orator); no marks; prob. sterling; $45.00 – 75.00.

Plate 24

Plate 25

Plate 26

Plate 27

Plate 28

Plate 29: James Garfield, (President); Gorham; $50.00 – 80.00.

Plate 29

— Military Men —

Plate 30: Gen. Maxmillian; untraced mark; $100.00 – 150.00; probably Gen. Custer (Little Big Horn); Shepard; $100.00 – 150.00; Pedro Del Tovar, untraced mark; $100.00 – 150.00.

Plate 31: Reverse of Plate 30.

Plate 30   Plate 31

Plate 32: Sir William Johnson, (French & Indian War Colonel); no manuf. mark; $50.00 – 65.00.

Plate 33: Gen. Robert E. Lee; Gorham, $150.00 – 250.00; Lee Monument; Gettysburg back; Watson; $50.00 – 100.00.

Plate 34: Gen. Robert E. Lee; Shepard, $100.00 – 150.00; Gen. John Brown Gordon, (Georgia Confederacy); Shepard; $100.00 – 150.00.

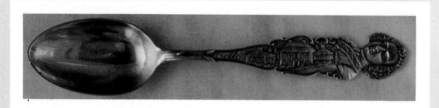

Plate 32

Plate 33

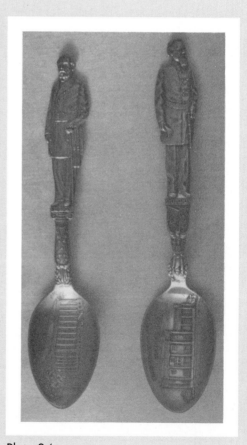

Plate 34

Plate 35: Gen. Wooster; (note: name is upside down); no mark, prob. sterling; F.L.Wilson; $50.00 – 100.00.

Plate 36: Gen. Grant, (President); Shiebler; $40.00 – 75.00.

Plate 37: Admiral Perry; Gorham; $75.00 – 115.00.

Plate 35

Plate 36

Plate 37

— Fictional Characters —

The Salem Witch spoon has been credited with starting the souvenir spoon movement in the United States. Character spoons have been available since the 1500s, but a combination of events including unusual spoons from Europe, an oversupply of precious silver, modern technology, and generally prosperous conditions seemed to have coalesced at this point in history. The Witch spoon and good sales were the final sparks which set events in motion.

Plate 38: Uncle Sam; Manchester/Baker; $40.00 – 75.00; Uncle Sam; J. Karr; $100.00 – 150.00; Uncle Sam; Alvin; $100.00 – 200.00.

Plate 39: Uncle Sam, demi; J. Karr; $30.00 – 60.00; Washington; R. Harris & Co., ca. 1891; $50.00 – 80.00; Uncle Sam; no manuf, mark; demi; $30.00 – 60.00.

Plate 38

Plate 39

Plate 40: Uncle Sam, full figure enameled; no manuf. mark; ca. 1909; $250.00 – 325.00.

Plate 41: Salem Witch, first edition; pat. March 3, 1891; Daniel Low; $30.00 – 50.00; available in two sizes and with different bowls; demi, $20.00 – 30.00.

Plate 42: Salem Witch, second edition; Daniel Low; $40.00 – 100.00; different sizes and different bowls available.

Plate 43: Rip Van Winkle; from Johnstown, ca. 1891; $40.00 – 80.00.

Plate 41

Plate 40

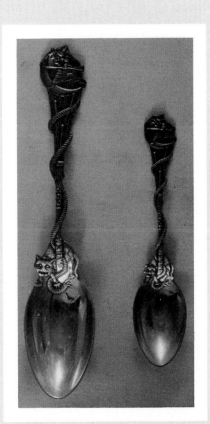

Plate 42

Plate 43

Plate 44: Rip Van Winkle; bowl has cats shooting at mountains, reads "Cats Kill Mountains" rebus; Watson; $150.00 – 225.00.

Plate 45: Rip Van Winkle; Durgin; $40.00 – 70.00.

Plate 46: King, 9.125"; Gorham; #H79; $500.00+.

Plate 47: Queen, 9.125"; Gorham; #H78; $500.00+.

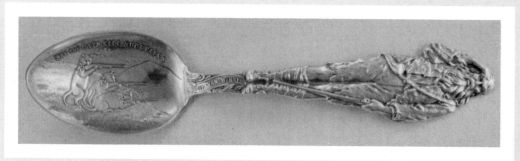

Plate 44

Plate 45

Plate 46

Plate 47

Plate 48: Knickerbocker, (Washington Irving pen name and book); Durgin; $25.00 – 45.00.

Plate 49: Moll Pitcher, (a fortune telling psychic popularized by American writer Whittier); Durgin, ca. 1891; $20.00 – 45.00.

Plate 50: Priscilla, (from the poem by John Alden); Durgin, ca. 1892; $20.00 – 30.00.

Plate 51: Evangeline, from the poem by Longfellow; Durgin; $30.00 – 50.00.

Plate 52: Miles Standish, (Pilgrim leader popularized by Longfellow); Durgin; $30.00 – 50.00.

Plate 49

Plate 51

Plate 48

Plate 50

Plate 52

Plate 53: Watson and Newell Co. catalog, ca. 1900 – 1910.

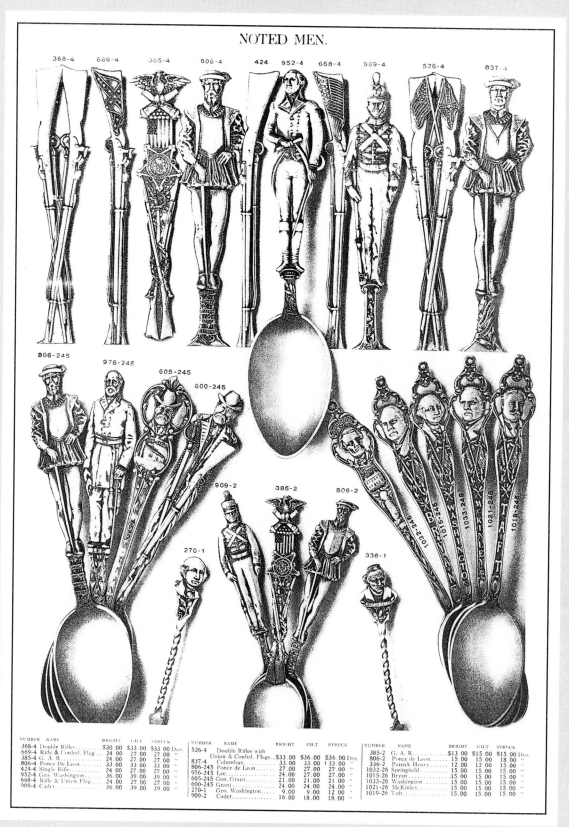

The First Americans

By the 1890s, the Wild West had been "tamed." The American Indians who had inhabited these vast areas had either been killed, absorbed by the new culture, or relegated to reservations. Until this time, the dominant opinion had been that the Indians were basically savages and had little to offer the country. Now that the native Indians were no longer perceived as being a threat, the attitudes of the "white man" changed.

The late Victorians rediscovered the important Indian cultures and they also rediscovered that the Indians had played a very important part in the affairs of the United States. Many cities had important Indians in their history. Numerous chiefs and ordinary Indians had provided substantial support for the western settlers. Thousands of different varieties of spoons were made to honor the "noble savages." It is also very common to find part of a spoon honoring Indians and another part a different subject.

Indian spoons are one of the most common themes of souvenir spoons and are highly collectible. In spoon collecting we have different types of Indian spoons. The first is those spoons made by established silver spoon manufacturers to honor the generic Indian and specific important tribal chieftains. Second we find spoons made by Indians.

The manufacturers were very attuned to the public perception of the American Indian and created their spoons to cater to these perceptions. This is the more dominant theme and silver manufacturers have created a number of exquisite spoons.

Collectors particularly like the full figural Indian spoons and a number of varieties are available. But the collector of this genre should not overlook the many other varieties which picture Indians as part of a series of themes. In addition there are some spoons of this genre which are quite unusual such as the Indian burial mound which is a modern day anthropological site.

The Southwest tribes (Hopi and Zuni) learned silversmithing from Mexican silversmiths and then created their own traditions. Most of their original silverwork was jewelry for their tribe. But as the number of travelers increased and the souvenir spoon movement became more important, both the new Indian trade schools and established silversmiths created spoons for the tourists.

The Fred Harvey Company catered to railroad travelers and began subletting custom silver work to Indian trades people for sale in their souvenir shops. Much of the flatware made by the southwest tribes was for sale to eastern travelers as the Indians themselves did not use silver flatware. Furthermore, most of the symbols which we find on spoons from this region have no meaning to the Indians themselves but were placed on these pieces because that is what the eastern travelers expected Indian silver to look like. Collectors can now find a great many silver objects of all kinds that were made by various Indian tribes. Relatively little documentation exists on early Indian silversmithing traditions and much of their silver is not marked to indicate its source or purity. Typically they used either American or Mexican silver coins, but as they became wealthier they bought flatting equipment which greatly simplified their job. Many of these objects show very fine craftsmanship and they are an important part of the American folk art tradition. These spoons are distinctive.

Readers are cautioned not to assume that all unmarked spoons are Indian-made since the vast majority are not. Some American spoon manufacturers even began to imitate the Indian-made pieces using mechanical equipment. One should look for evidence of hand work to confirm that a piece is Indian-made. Furthermore Japan has even tried to produce Indian look-alike souvenir spoons, but these are generally marked with the word "Japan."

Totem poles are heraldic devices of the Northwestern Indian cultures and are used to honor an important person or to pass on tribal lore and legend. The original poles were carved from cedar trees and painted with natural ingredients. The silver totem pole spoons were made by both established silver manufacturers and by the Tlingit or Haida Indians and sold to visiting tourists. Most of these latter pieces are not marked as to purity or origin but show unmistakable evidence of hand-worked manufacturing but common threads run through all the totem poles and even the handworked ones were made repeatedly.

Ironically, most of the original totem poles which were made of wood have disintegrated with age and one of the few proofs of their existence are the pictures and silver spoon souvenirs.

— Manufactured Indian Spoons —

Plate 54: Indian with oar-heavy, ("Buckskin Charlie"); not traced (DJ); poss. Canada ; $150.00 – 200.00.

Plate 55: Indian with bow; National Silver Co.; engraved "12-11-11"; $150.00 – 200.00.

Plate 56: Indians with crossed arms; Meyer Bros., gold washed bowl, eng. "10/9/07"; $125.00 – 175.00; Fessenden; plain bowl; $60.00 – 80.00.

Plate 57: Indian with spear; Shiebler; $120.00 – 200.00.

Plate 54

Plate 55

Plate 56

Plate 57

Plate 58: Full figural with fancy headress; untraced; $100.00 – 150.00.

Plate 59: Partial handle full figures. Durgin; $50.00 – 85.00; Garden of the Gods; Deacon Jewelry; $80.00 – 150.00; Yosemite; Paye & Baker; $125.00 – 175.00.

Plate 60: Standing Indians, with bow; San Gabriel Mission; no manuf. mark; $75.00 – 125.00; with tomahawk, Weidlich; $75.00 – 150.00; with spear, Meyer Bros.; $75.00 – 125.00.

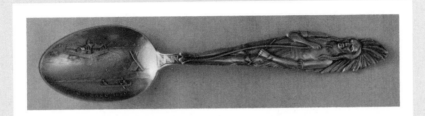

Plate 58

Plate 59

Plate 60

Plate 61: Standing Indians; Rock Springs; Mechanics; $80.00 – 115.00; Portland, symbols in bowl; untraced; $85.00 – 150.00; Rapid City; National Silver Co.; (Squaw on back) $150.00 – 200.00.

Plate 62: Indian with tomahawk; Shepard; $150.00 – 200.00; (front of spoon is a full-figured cowboy).

Plate 63: Detail, Sacajawea, (interpreter for Lewis & Clark expedition); Meyer Bros; $50.00 – 70.00.

Plate 61

Plate 62

Plate 63

Plate 64: Three dimensional Indian with corn; Mechanics; $25.00 – 45.00.

Plate 65: Indian with spear and tomahawk, Royal Gorge in bowl; National Silver Co.; $150.00 – 200.00.

Plate 66: Reverse of above, squaw with papoose.

Plate 67: Detroit waterfront; no manuf. mark; $75.00 – 125.00; plain bowl; Paye & Baker; $50.00 – 75.00; Spokane Bridge; Deacon; $65.00 – 100.00.

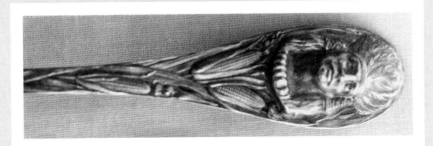

Plate 64

Plate 65

Plate 66

Plate 67

Plate 68: Kneeling Indian; Manchester/Baker; (available with many different bowls and sizes); $30.00 – 75.00.

Plate 69: Indian scout, (aka setting sun); Paye & Baker; $40.00 – 75.00; folded arms; Tammen; $50.00 – 80.00; fancy headress; Paye & Baker; $75.00 – 125.00.

Plate 70: Niagara Falls; no manuf. mark; $40.00 – 80.00; Chief Ouray; Gorham; $250.00 – 350.00; no manuf. mark; prob. Gorham; $45.00 – 75.00.

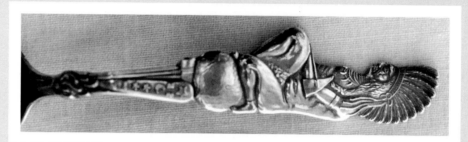

Plate 68

Plate 69

Plate 70

Plate 71: Geronimo, San Xavier; Wendall Manufacturing; $75.00 – 125.00; Two Feather; S.D. Childs & Co.; $45.00 – 65.00. (Silver plated advertising)

Plate 72: Shabbona, "The White Man's Friend;" Gorham, $65.00 – 100.00; full figural princess; Canon City; no manuf. mark; $150.00 – 175.00.

Plate 73: Maid of the Mist (Niagara Falls tour boat); no manuf. mark; $150.00 – 200.00.

Plate 71

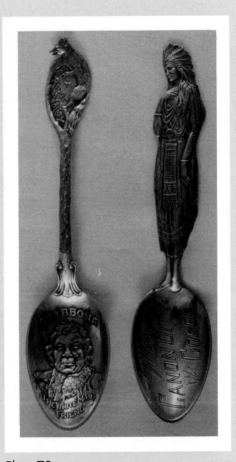

Plate 72

Plate 73

Plate 74: Indian in canoe; Lunt; (available with different bowls); $20.00 – 45.00.

Plate 75: Indian rider; Lunt; $40.00 – 65.00; Niagara Falls; no manuf. mark; $50.00 – 60.00.

Plate 76: Indian squaw, enameled bowl; Watson; $200.00 – 300.00+.

Plate 74

Plate 75

Plate 76

Plate 77: Chief Oshkosh; Towle for Birely & Sons, retailer; $30.00 – 65.00.

Plate 78: Niagara Falls, White Canoe; demi; no manuf. mark; $40.00 – 75.00; Niagara Falls; no manuf. mark; $45.00 – 60.00; Hopi House; Shepard; $40.00 – 70.00.

Plate 79: Small pedestal Indian; Lunt; $40.00 – 60.00; White Canoe; Mechanics; $60.00 – 75.00; three-quarter-standing Indian; Watson; $60.00 – 75.00.

Plate 77

Plate 78

Plate 79

Plate 80: Covered wagon; Reilly Curtis & Co.; $30.00 – 60.00; electric tower, Indian on a globe; Shiebler; $125.00 – 150.00.

Plate 81: Eskimo ice fishing; Meyer Bros.; $125.00 – 200.00; (Eskimo woman and child); Meyer Bros; $125.00 – 200.00.

Plate 82: Engraved, Mound Cemetery; Marietta, Ohio; these mounds are very ancient; Wallace; Irving pattern, ca. 1900; $30.00 – 40.00.

Plate 80

Plate 81

Plate 82

Plate 83: Ogontz; Dominick, 1903; $30.00 – 50.00.

Plate 84: Detail, engraved, Princess Angeline; Seattle; totem pole handle; $40.00 – 60.00.

Plate 85: Indian lovers; Paye & Baker; $80.00 – 125.00; Indian maiden; Spokane; Meyer Bros.; $80.00 – 125.00.

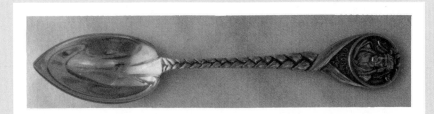

Plate 83

Plate 84

Plate 85

Plate 86: Detail, painted enamels, Indians; plain bowl; Shepard; $50.00 – 90.00 each.

Plate 87: Chief Seattle, enamel portrait; Shepard; $150.00 – 200.00.

Plate 88: Pottery maker, New Mexico, plain bowl; unidentified maker; $15.00 – 25.00.

Plate 89: Detail (embossed), pottery maker; Tammen; $125.00 – 175.00.

Plate 86

Plate 87

Plate 88

Plate 89

Plate 90: Indian pottery carrier; Fred Harvey; $80.00 – 125.00; pottery maker, see detail; Tammen; $125.00 – 175.00; pottery carrier, plain bowl; Meyer Bros.; $50.00 – 75.00.

Plate 91: Large silver pot; (note: very large three-dimensional pot, photographed at angle to show dimension); Gorham; $300.00 – 400.00.

Plate 92: Papoose; Watson; $60.00 – 95.00.

Plate 93: Blanket weaver; Hirsch & Oppenheimer; $50.00 – 85.00.

Plate 90

Plate 91

Plate 92

Plate 93

— Spoons Made By Indians —

Plate 94: Swastika; $35.00 – 70.00. Middle spoon: (note that the top sun design is very three-dimensional), $20.00 – 40.00. Navajo Indian profile; $35.00 – 65.00.

Plate 95: Turquoise cabochon; $25.00 – 40.00. Mule, very unusual design; $25.00 – 40.00.

Plate 96: Stylized animal; $25.00 – 40.00.

Plate 94

Plate 95

Plate 96

Note: The swastika was an ancient symbol of good luck to the Indians of the Southwest and most of Latin America. It was also found in several Asian cultures. It became a symbol of disgust after it was used by the Nazis during World War II when it became associated with the atrocities perpetrated by that regime.

Plate 97: Feather spoon; $20.00 – 30.00.

Plate 98: Eagle with turquoise cabochon; $25.00 – 60.00; smaller eagle with turquoise; $20.00 – 35.00.

Plate 99: Round bowl, hand pounded; $25.00 – 50.00; salmon; Sitka; $25.00 – 50.00; flattened top, hand pounded bowl; $25.00 – 50.00.

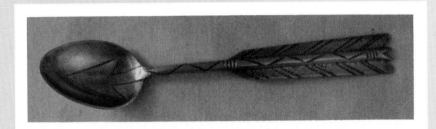

Plate 97

Plate 98

Plate 99

Plate 100: Cut-out head figure over filigree work; $25.00 – 45.00.

Plate 101: Yei figure; marked Francis Jones; $35.00 – 60.00; stylized figure; unmarked; $20.00 – 30.00.

Plate 102: Note three-dimensional sun design; $25.00 – 40.00.

Plate 103: Poorly executed design, probably a school project; $10.00 – 15.00.

Plate 100

Plate 101

Plate 102

Plate 103

Plate 104: Totem pole; $30.00 – 50.00; whale; $25.00 – 50.00; salmon; $25.00 – 50.00; totem pole; $30.00 – 60.00.

Plate 105: Turquoise mounted in male finial; marked sterling; $20.00 – 50.00; large oval-shaped turquoise under crossed arrows; no mark; $20.00 – 50.00.

Plate 104

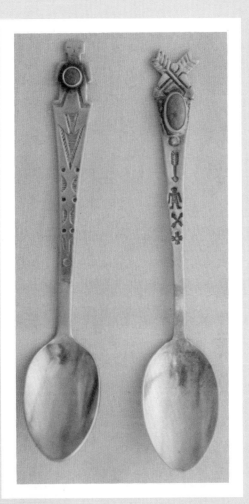

Plate 105

> **Note:** The large number of stamped designs were for the benefit of the Eastern tourists (the likely buyers) to meet their perception of what an Indian spoon should look like. Most were probably sold through Fred Harvey souvenir shops.

Plate 106: Arrowhead feather spoons; $20.00 – 40.00 each.

Plate 107: Totem pole; $30.00 – 60.00.

Plate 108: Totem pole; $30.00 – 70.00.

Plate 109: Totem pole, $20.00 – 40.00; totem pole, Alaska; $30.00 – 50.00.

Plate 106

Plate 107

Plate 108

Plate 109

Plate 110: Watson and Newell Co. catalog, ca. 1900 – 1910.

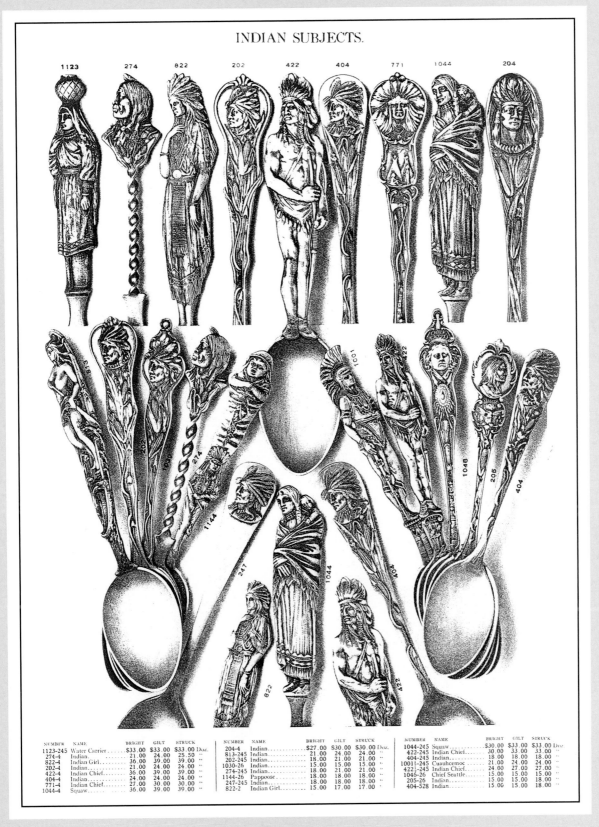

INDIAN SUBJECTS.

NUMBER	NAME	BRIGHT	GILT	STRUCK
1123-245	Water Carrier	$33.00	$33.00	$33.00 Doz.
274-4	Indian	21.00	24.00	25.50 "
822-4	Indian Girl	36.00	39.00	39.00 "
202-4	Indian	21.00	24.00	24.00 "
422-4	Indian Chief	36.00	39.00	39.00 "
404-4	Indian	24.00	24.00	24.00 "
771-4	Indian Chief	27.00	30.00	30.00 "
1044-4	Squaw	36.00	39.00	39.00 "

NUMBER	NAME	BRIGHT	GILT	STRUCK
204-4	Indian	$27.00	$30.00	$30.00 Doz.
813-245	Indian	21.00	24.00	24.00 "
202-245	Indian	18.00	21.00	21.00 "
1030-26	Indian	15.00	15.00	15.00 "
274-245	Indian	18.00	21.00	21.00 "
1144-26	Pappoose	18.00	18.00	18.00 "
247-245	Indian	18.00	18.00	18.00 "
822-2	Indian Girl	15.00	17.00	17.00 "

NUMBER	NAME	BRIGHT	GILT	STRUCK
1044-245	Squaw	$30.00	$33.00	$33.00 Doz.
422-245	Indian Chief	30.00	33.00	33.00 "
404-245	Indian	18.00	18.00	18.00 "
1001½-245	Cuauhcemoc	21.00	24.00	24.00 "
422½-245	Indian Chief	24.00	27.00	27.00 "
1046-26	Chief Seattle	15.00	15.00	15.00 "
205-26	Indian	15.00	15.00	18.00 "
404-528	Indian	15.00	15.00	18.00 "

Plate 110

45

Taming the Wilderness

The cowboy image is usually a popular fantasy of the eastern United States writers' minds. Writers in the 1890s produced numerous novels and stories that glorified cowboys and the Western way of life. Any actual relationship to real life was purely coincidental. The actual life of the cowboy was hard, tough, dirty, and lonely work. But these novelists painted fanciful word portraits of the cowboy's life. The novels, movies, and television shows have had such a powerful effect that we still think about cowboys as they portrayed them. Most of the spoons of this genre show this popular image of these hard-working men and women.

Cowboy spoons are very highly collectible. For the most part, they are relatively rare and the ones that do exist are of exceptionally nice design. Spoons of cowgirls are even rarer than those of cowboys.

Plate 111: Hirsch & Oppenheimer; $150.00 – 225.00.

Plate 112: Reverse of Plate 111.

Plate 113: "Broncho (sic) rider;" J. Mayer Bros; $55.00 – 90.00.

Plate 114: Reverse of Plate 113.

Plate 111

Plate 112

Plate 113

Plate 114

Plate 115: Ropin' cowboy; Watson; $150.00 – 200.00.

Plate 116: Reverse of Plate 115.

Plate 117: Cow roper; engraved Tijuana, Mexico; Anderson Jewelry; $60.00 – 120.00.

Plate 118: Mounted cowgirl; Watson; $90.00 – 150.00.

Plate 115

Plate 116

Plate 117

Plate 118

Plate 119: Steer roper; Meyer Bros; $75.00 – 100.00.

Plate 120: Finial rider; no manuf. mark; $60.00 – 75.00.

Plate 121: Cowboy front, Indian back (pictured in Indian chapter, Plate 62); Shepard; $150.00 – 200.00.

Plate 122: Buffalo Bill Cody; Weidlich; $50.00 – 75.00.

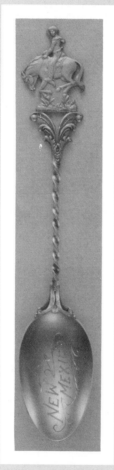

Plate 120

Plate 122

Plate 119

Plate 121

Plate 123: Lady rider, engraved picture of Mt. Rainier; Meyer Bros; $200.00 – 250.00.

Plate 124: Reverse of Plate 123.

Plate 125: Cowboy finial; Mechanics; $50.00 – 80.00.

Plate 126: Reverse of Plate 125.

Plate 127: Generic farmer, figural; Meyer Bros; $75.00 – 125.00.

Plate 124

Plate 126

Plate 125

Plate 123

Plate 127

Plate 128: Scranton; SSMC; $50.00 – 90.00; remake, "1977 spooners convention, 7/8-10/1977"; no manuf. mark; $50.00 – 90.00; Denver, Hirsch & Oppenheimer; $175.00 – 225.00.

Plate 129: Fine Arts Bldg, Calif. Mid-Winter Fair; no manuf. mark; $75.00 – 125.00; Denver Capitol; no manuf. mark; $40.00 – 75.00. Note: silver plated versions are less than $20.00.

Plate 128

Plate 129

Plate 130: Grass Valley; Meyer Bros; $125.00 – 175.00; Old Faithful Inn; Mechanics; $100.00 – 150.00; steam shovel; Manchester/Baker; $125.00 – 150.00.

Plate 131: Ridin' and shootin' cowboy on the range; Watson; $175.00 – 200.00.

Plate 132: Reverse of Plate 131.

Plate 130

Plate 131

Plate 132

Plate 133: Engraved mule; Deacon Jewelry; $50.00 – 75.00; Santa Barbara mission; no manuf. mark; $30.00 – 60.00.

Plate 134: Struck-it-rich, copper; Deacon Jewelry; $20.00 – 60.00; large nugget; Hirsch & Oppenheimer; $100.00 – 125.00; Denver Capitol; Hirsch & Oppenheimer; $75.00 – 100.00.

Plate 133

Plate 134

Plate 135: Denver; no manuf. mark; $50.00 – 70.00; miner at rest; Hirsch & Oppenheimer; $75.00 – 90.00.

Plate 136: Demi, Los Angeles; SSMC; $20.00 – 40.00; demi, plain bowl, Meyer Bros.; $30.00 – 40.00; demi, Denver; Hirsch & Oppenheimer; $30.00 – 50.00.

Plate 137: Gold miner, artificial $50 gold piece; no manuf. mark; $150.00 – 200.00.

Plate 135

Plate 136

Plate 137

Plate 138: "El Dorado," Administration Building; $20.00 – 40.00.

Plate 139: Miner pan; many different variations are available; $15.00 – 50.00. (Shovel bowls are interesting variations.)

Plate 140: Mine worker; not traced, prob. Homer; $50.00 – 75.00; windlass, mechanical with chain that moves; no manuf. mark; $125.00 – 175.00.

Plate 138

Plate 139

Plate 140

Plate 141: Watson and Newell Co. catalog, ca. 1900 – 1910.

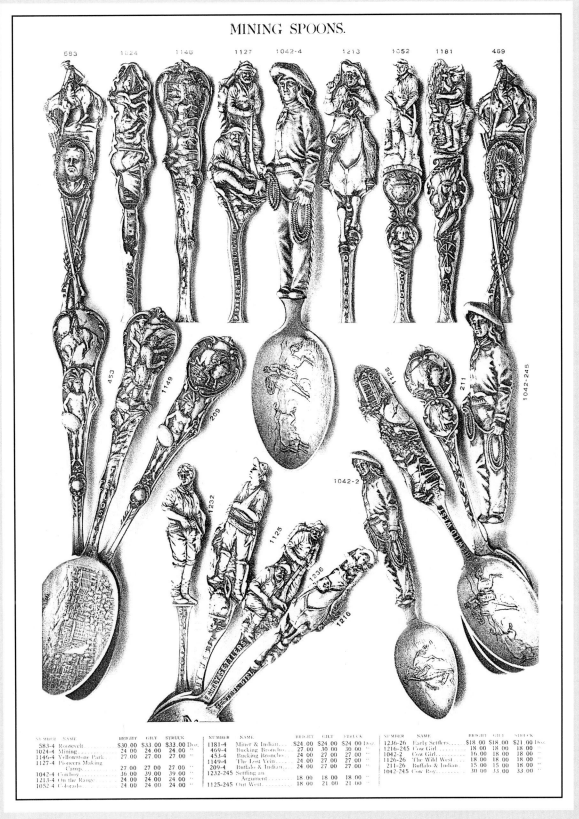

Plate 141

Plate 142: Watson and Newell Co. catalog, ca. 1900 – 1910.

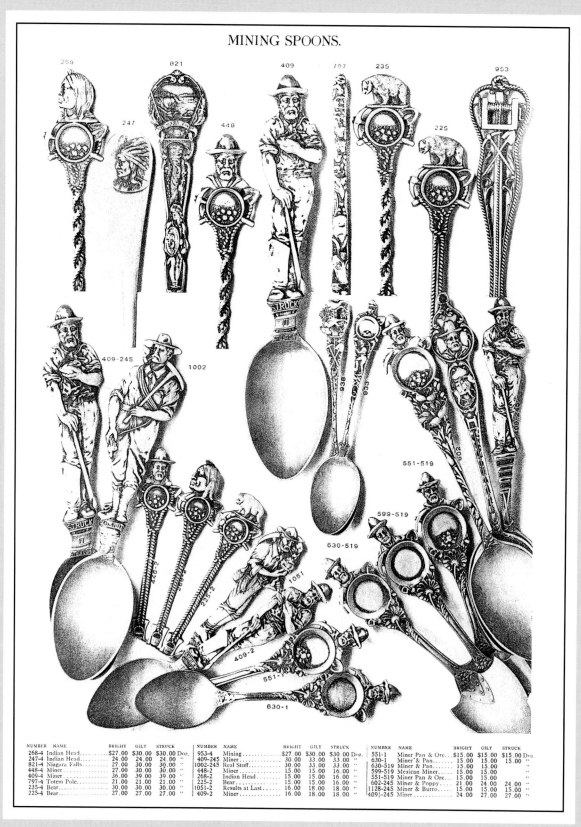

MINING SPOONS.

NUMBER	NAME	BRIGHT	GILT	STRUCK	NUMBER	NAME	BRIGHT	GILT	STRUCK	NUMBER	NAME	BRIGHT	GILT	STRUCK
268-4	Indian Head	$27.00	$30.00	$30.00 Doz.	953-4	Mining	$27.00	$30.00	$30.00 Doz.	551-1	Miner Pan & Ore	$15.00	$15.00	$15.00 Doz.
247-4	Indian Head	24.00	24.00	24.00 "	409-245	Miner	30.00	33.00	33.00 "	630-1	Miner & Pan	15.00	15.00	15.00 "
821-4	Niagara Falls	27.00	30.00	30.00 "	1002-245	Real Stuff	30.00	33.00	33.00 "	630-519	Miner & Pan	15.00	15.00	"
448-4	Miner	27.00	30.00	30.00 "	448-2	Miner	15.00	15.00	16.00 "	599-519	Mexican Miner	15.00	15.00	"
409-4	Miner	36.00	39.00	39.00 "	268-2	Indian Head	15.00	15.00	16.00 "	551-519	Miner Pan & Ore	15.00	15.00	"
797-4	Totem Pole	21.00	21.00	21.00 "	225-2	Bear	15.00	15.00	16.00 "	602-245	Miner & Poppy	21.00	24.00	24.00 "
235-4	Bear	30.00	30.00	30.00 "	1051-2	Results at Last	16.00	18.00	18.00 "	1128-245	Miner & Burro	15.00	15.00	15.00 "
225-4	Bear	27.00	27.00	27.00 "	409-2	Miner	16.00	18.00	18.00 "	409]-245	Miner	24.00	27.00	27.00 "

Plate 142

From Sea to Shining Sea

Every country has many beautiful sights and much gorgeous scenery, but the United States is a huge land that has been blessed with thousands of beautiful and unusual works of nature. It is simply not possible to show all the spoons honoring her many natural wonders. We find numerous types and varieties of spoons for all the major tourist attractions plus we find a number of spoons honoring lesser-known sites, scenes, parks, and other natural wonders.

Niagara Falls is probably the most widely visited natural waterfall in the world. The majestic volcano mountains of Oregon and Washington are also frequently found on spoons. The vast Alaskan wilderness gives us many exciting and unusual pieces and the lush islands of Hawaii provide some contrasting examples. Pikes Peak and the Garden of the Gods in Colorado were common tourist attractions which showed unusual examples of natural erosion. Of course, all the major parks eventually had silver spoons available to visiting tourists. Spoons showing picturesque settings are available from every state. A travelogue of the United States in spoons would be a remarkable exhibit.

— Mountains —

Plate 144: Engraved, Mt. Baker, totem pole handle; Joseph Meyer & Bros.; $40.00 – 60.00; engraved; Mt. Rainier; Towle; $30.00 – 50.00.

Plate 145: Summit of Pikes Peak; embossed Denver capitol; $25.00 – 40.00.

Plate 144

Plate 145

Plate 146: Three engraved views of Mt. Hood, Oregon. Notice both the similarities and differences and the various artistic renderings of the engravings. The Northwest mountain views are among the most common mountain engravings available. Top, Wallace; $30.00 – 50.00; middle, Shepard wavy handle; GWB; $30.00 – 60.00; bottom, Whiting; Imperial Queen pattern; $30.00 – 50.00.

Plate 147: Enlarged detail of Wallace spoon.

Plate 148: Unusual Indian-made, engraved; Royal Gorge, Colorado; $35.00 – 75.00.

Plate 146

Plate 148

Plate 147

Plate 149: Engraved; Sugar Loaf Mountain; Watson; $30.00 – 50.00.

Plate 150: There are a great many spoons depicting scenes from Pikes Peak, Colorado; engraved summit of Pikes Peak; Shepard wavy handle; $30.00 – 50.00; Pikes Peak – Garden of the Gods; Reed & Barton; $30.00 – 50.00.

Plate 149

Plate 150

Plate 151: Demi; mule finial on handmade twisted stem with embossed bowl of the signal station on Pikes Peak; no mark; $10.00 – 25.00.

Plate 152: High Rock Spring, Saratoga, N.Y.; unidentified manuf., prob. Shepard; $30.00 – 50.00.

Plate 153: Engraved; "I helped to build Pikes Peak;" Shepard $30.00 – 50.00

Plate 152

Plate 151

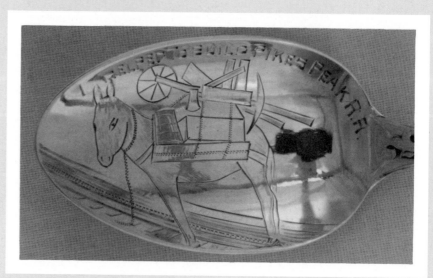

Plate 153

Plate 154: Adirondacks; Towle; $40.00 – 70.00.

Plate 155: White Horse, Vermont, dog sled, engraved bowl; Joseph Meyer; $75.00 – 125.00; White Horse, Vermont, engraved bowl, dog sled, seal, and polar bear; Pat 5/21/1901; $60.00 – 100.00.

Plate 156: Colorado, Gateway to Garden of the Gods; no manuf. mark; $40.00 – 75.00.

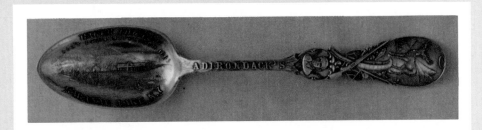

Plate 154

Plate 155

Plate 156

— Waterfalls —

Niagara Falls is the most common waterfall pictured on spoons and there are an estimated 900+ varieties of these spoons. They range in value from $20.00 – 500.00. Minehaha Falls is the next most common set of falls pictured with numerous examples.

Plate 157: Square shovel bowl with Indian finial; the Indian face is bronzed over the silver; the bowl is engraved; Codding Bros; $150.00 – 200.00+.

Plate 158: Niagara Falls; W.E.Glenn & Sons; $50.00 – 75.00.

Plate 159: Mendenhall's Glacier, Juneau, Alaska; Joseph Meyer; $20.00 – 30.00.

Plate 157

Plate 158

Plate 159

Plate 160: Engraved, Passaic Falls, Paterson, New Jersey; Chantilly pattern; Gorham; $30.00 – 50.00.

Plate 161: Engraved, Natural Bridge, Santa Cruz, Calif.; unidentified manuf.; $30.00 – 50.00.

Plate 162: Niagara Falls; Watson; $20.00 – 25.00.

Plate 160

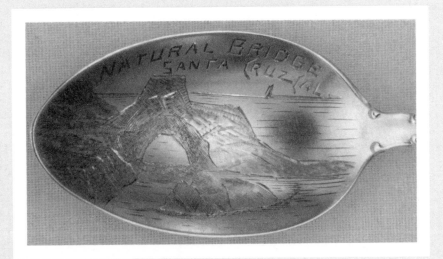

Plate 161

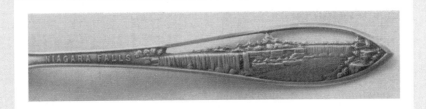

Plate 162

— Parks —

All the federal parks are pictured on spoons. In addition, many state and local parks are also available. The more popular the park, the greater number and variety of spoons that can be found.

Plate 163: Yellowstone; unidentified manuf.; $40.00 – 75.00.

Plate 164: Yellowstone, Great Falls; Robbins; $15.00 – 30.00; family group; Robbins; $15.00 – 30.00; bear; Tammen; $15.00 – 20.00.

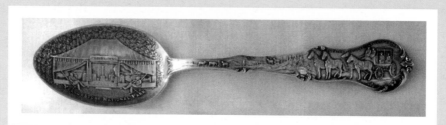

Plate 163

Plate 164

Plate 165: Chimney Rock, Wisconsin Dells; $10.00 – 20.00.

Plate 166: Engraved, Deer Park, Belle Isle, Michigan; no manuf. mark, $30.00 – 40.00; engraved, Washington Park, Quincy, Illinois; Mothers pattern; Gorham; $30.00 – 40.00.

Plate 167: Jackson Hole, Grand Teton, demi; unidentified manuf., $10.00 – 20.00; Royal Gorge, Colorado, demi; unidentified manuf.; $10.00 – 20.00; Great Smoky Mountains, demi; Tammen; $10.00 – 20.00; Glacier National Park, demi; unidentified manuf.; $10.00 – 20.00.

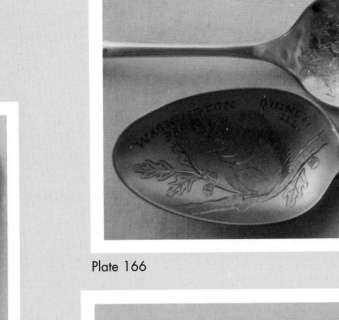

Plate 166

Plate 165

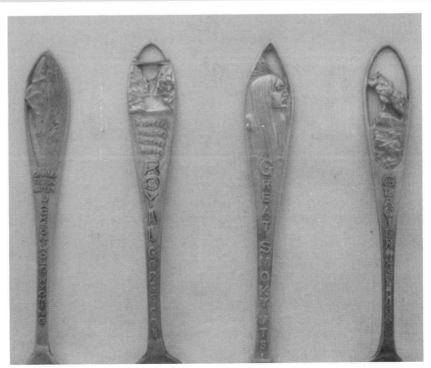

Plate 167

Plate 168: Engraved, Earlington Park, Sulphur Springs; Mechanics; $30.00 – 50.00; engraved, Krug Park, St. Joseph, Missouri, ca. 1905; Mechanics, $30.00 – 50.00.

Plate 169: Plymouth Rock, Pilgrim Landing; Towle; Gooding Bros; $20.00 – 35.00.

Plate 170: Bryce Canyon, sunburst style bowl; Robbins; $20.00 – 40.00.

Plate 168

Plate 170

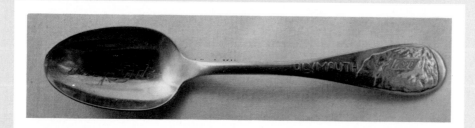

Plate 169

— Alaska, Hawaii, Catalina Island —

Alaska, Hawaii, and Catalina Island seemed to be more exotic to travelers than locations on the continent and they continue to attract more attention from collectors also. (More Alaska spoons are shown in the Indian chapters.)

Plate 171: Miner pan bowl; Alaska; unidentified manuf.; $25.00 – 40.00.

Plate 172: Unusual Alaska souvenir ice cream fork; Meyer Bros.; $50.00 – 100.00; enameled bowl, Hilo, Hawaii; Robbins; $75.00 – 125.00.

Plate 173: Miner's pan bowl; Valdez, Alaska; unidentified manuf.; $50.00 – 75.00.

Plate 171

Plate 172

Plate 173

Plate 174: Tongs, Alaska; no manuf. mark; $30.00 – 50.00.

Plate 175: Billiken, "the God of the way things ought to be;" ivory carved Billiken; no manuf. mark; $40.00 – 95.00; Billiken; Alaska; J. Mayer; $30.00 – 50.00.

Plate 176: Unusual enameled Pele, Goddess of Fire; $200.00+.

Plate 177: Actual Hawaiian coin bowl; Shreve; $150.00 – 225.00.

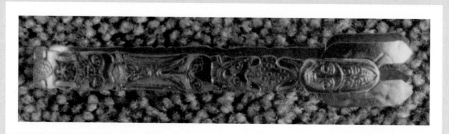

Plate 174

Plate 175

Plate 176

Plate 177

Plate 178: Catalina Island; Robbins; $20.00 – 25.00.

Plate 179: Demi, handmade and engraved spoon; Honoulu; no manuf. mark; $30.00 – 75.00.

Plate 180: Full figural Hawaiian fisherman with surf board scene, demi; Mechanics; $25.00 – 50.00; hand made with Hawaiian coin bowl, twisty stem and enameled finial; H. Culman (HC 1909 – 1917); Honolulu, Hawaii; $200.00 – 300.00.

Plate 181: Fork and spoon set; Watson (rare pennant W mark); $150.00 – 200.00 set.

Plate 178

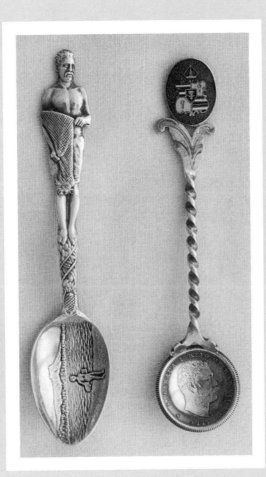

Plate 179   Plate 180   Plate 181

Plate 182: Various Catalina spoons. Left to right: no manuf. mark; $35.00 – 50.00; Shepard; $40.00 – 60.00; no manuf. mark; $40.00 – 60.00; no manuf. mark; $40.00 – 60.00; Manchester/Baker; $40.00 – 60.00; (upper), no manuf. mark; $30.00 – 40.00; Manchester/Baker; $40.00 – 60.00; Mechanics; 40.00 – 75.00.

Plate 182

Plate 183: California, spreader and spoon; Shreve; $50.00 – 100.00 set.

Plate 184: California, bon bon spoons and fork; Shreve; $125.00 – 200.00 set.

Plate 185: California, spoon, pastry fork, fork; Mechanics; $125.00 – 175.00 set.

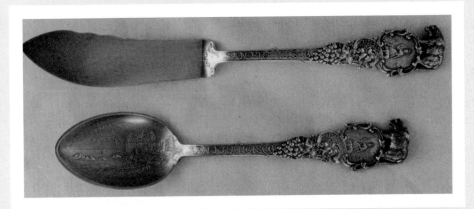

Plate 183

Plate 184

Plate 185

Plate 186: Three pieces from Catalina Island; Watson; $40.00 – 70.00 each.

Plate 187: San Francisco skyline spoons, different pictures in bowl depicting the disastrous earthquake and fire which consumed the city in April, 1906; Watson; $500.00 – 700.00 set.

Plate 186

Plate 187

Building a Nation

Visitors have always enjoyed historical buildings. Until the 1890s, most old buildings were simply razed when they no longer served their intended purposes. But just before the turn of the century, groups of civic-minded citizens, women's civic organizations in particular, realized the destruction of these old buildings was really the destruction of our history. Major attempts were made to preserve as many significant historic buildings as possible. But restoration is an expensive job, and one of the major ways to obtain the necessary money was to cater to tourists. Souvenirs were often the source of additional monetary funding for the restoration effort.

Old military forts which were once isolated outposts are often now in the centers of cities. Other early buildings often have rich and colorful pasts. The late Victorians loved to decorate their parks and public buildings with large bronze sculptures of local historical heroes. In spoon collecting we have many pieces showing these various historic buildings and some of the many monuments erected to honor local heroes.

Spoons depicting these time-honored monuments show great artistic qualities and provide a sense of history at the same time.

Plate 188: Point Comfort; Durgin; $30.00 – 50.00.

Plate 189: Engraved, Fort Sumter, early Civil War site; gold washed bowl; Towle; $25.00 – 50.00.

Plate 188

Plate 189

Plate 190: Sutters Fort, Calif., "first publicized discovery of gold, California"; Shepard; $25.00 – 50.00.

Plate 191: Alamo, Texas, (last stand for Davy Crockett et. al.); marked L.W.B.; $85.00 – 125.00.

Plate 192: Mount Vernon, (Washington's home); $30.00 – 50.00.

Plate 190

Plate 191

Plate 192

Plate 193: Christ Church near Mount Vernon; George & Betty Washington; Mechanics; $35.00 – 50.00.

Plate 194: Faneuil Hall, Boston, (pre-Revolutionary War meeting site); Homer; $50.00 – 75.00.

Plate 195: House of Betsy Ross, (maker of country's first flag); Robbins; $20.00 – 40.00

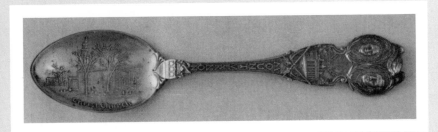

Plate 193

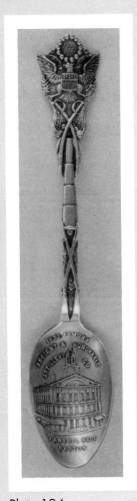

Plate 194

Plate 195

Plate 196: House of Seven Gables, (Longfellow home); no manuf. mark; not a true witch spoon; $20.00 – 50.00.

Plate 197: Engraved San Gabriel Mission; Marie Antoinette pattern, ca. 1905; Gorham; $40.00 – 75.00.

Plate 198: Postcard, bells of San Gabriel Mission.

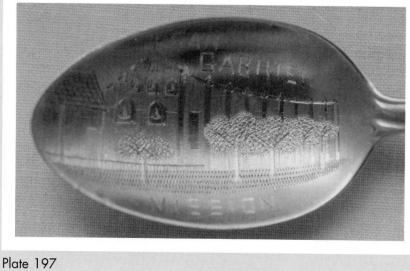

Plate 197

Plate 196

Plate 198

Plate 199: Postcard, Mission Santa Barbara.

Plate 200: Santa Barbara Mission; Paye & Baker; $75.00 – 140.00 set.

Plate 199

Plate 200

Plate 201: Engraved, Santa Barbara Mission; gold washed; LDA; $25.00 – 50.00.

Plate 202: Postcard, Old Mission, San Diego.

Plate 201

OLD MISSION, SAN DIEGO, CALIFORNIA. Founded 1769
The date palms in foreground and olive trees in adjoining grove (over a century old) are still vigorous.   The ripe olives produced here are used in the manufacture of "Old Mission" pure California Olive Oil and also for "Old Mission" Ripe Olives, two of the finest products of California

Plate 202

Plate 203: San Diego Mission ruins; silver plate; $10.00 – 15.00.

Plate 204: Engraved, old Meeting House; Old English pattern; Towle; $25.00 – 50.00.

Plate 205: Engraved, Old Spanish Palace; Versailles pattern, dated 3/2/05; Gorham; $45.00 – 75.00.

Plate 203

Plate 204

Plate 205

Plate 206: Tucson, Arizona, Mission San Xavier; Robbins; $20.00 – 40.00.

Plate 207: San Juan Capistrano, Calif., showing San Juan Mission; Robbins; $20.00 – 40.00.

Plate 208: Washington; R. Harris & Co.; 1891; $50.00 – 75.00.

Plate 209: Engraved, demi, Andrew Johnson's old tailor shop, (fame by association), Greeneville, Tennessee; $20.00 – 40.00.

Plate 206

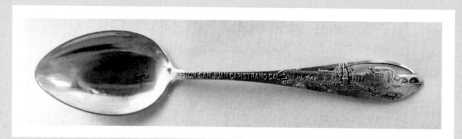

Plate 207

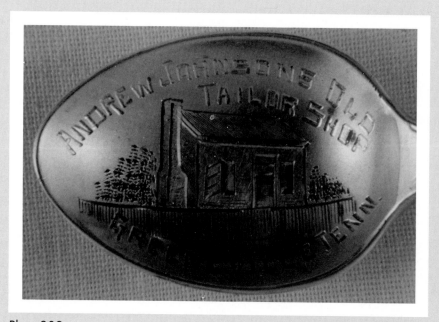

Plate 209

Plate 208

Plate 210: Engraved, old Kentucky home (many variations), Paducah, Ky.; Watson; $25.00 – 50.00.

Plate 211: Engraved, windmill, Lawrence, Kansas; Lancaster pattern; Gorham; $25.00 – 50.00.

Plate 212: Engraved, Centennial Monument; Edwardsville, Illinois; Manchester/Baker; $30.00 – 50.00.

Plate 210

Plate 211

Plate 212

Plate 213: Engraved, High Water Mark, Gettysburg; Baronial pattern; Frank Smith Co.; $40.00 – 75.00.

Plate 214: Washington cannon and Capitol; nice gold detailing; no manuf. mark; $60.00 – 100.00.

Plate 215: Engraved, Soldier and Sailor Monument; Cleveland; Georgian pattern, ca. 1905; Towle; $25.00 – 50.00.

Plate 216: Engraved, Francis Scott Key Memorial, (author of National Anthem), Frederick, Maryland; Art Deco hammered handle; SSMC; $30.00 – 60.00.

Plate 213

Plate 214

Plate 215

Plate 216

Plate 217: Engraved, Cemetery Gate, Vicksburg; Shepard; $30.00 – 60.00.

Plate 218: Engraved, Soldiers Monument; Worcester, Massachusetts; unidentified pattern; Alvin; $25.00 – 50.00.

Plate 219: Three engraved views of the Indianapolis Soldiers and Sailors Monument. These are all engraved by different artists and show variances in quality as well as perspective. Towle; gold wash bowl, Georgian/Grecian pattern, ca. 1889; $25.00 – 50.00; gold wash bowl; no manuf. mark; $20.00 – 40.00; no manuf. mark, $20.00 – 40.00.

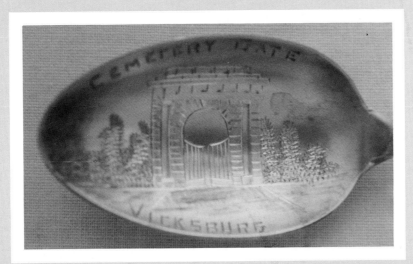

Plate 217

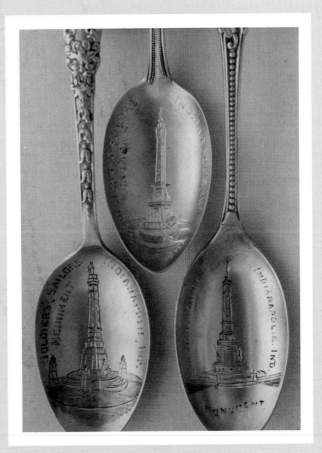

Plate 218   Plate 219

Americans at the Century Mark

In addition to an interest in events past, collectors of silver spoons also wanted spoons about contemporary people and events. Presidents were obvious choices and in addition to spoons honoring George Washington and Abraham Lincoln, we find that Grant, Garfield, and Cleveland were held in higher esteem then than they are now. McKinley was elected by the first "modern style" presidential campaign which was waged largely in the media. He did not campaign actively, but visitors would come to his house to hear speeches. One enterprising engraver gave us a number of examples of fine workmanship by engraving a bust of McKinley into spoon bowls. Teddy Roosevelt was a very colorful president and the subject of numerous spoons.

A number of lesser known politicians were also honored on spoons. Of significant interest are those spoons which comment on political controversies, usually through symbolism. These are a derivation of some old style English spoons from the 1700s which also used symbolism to comment on the monarchy.

Famous writers, business executives, and others in the public eye were often honored on spoons. Sometimes they arranged to produce them for their own benefit. When a famous person died, a spoon commemorating his life was sometimes created. These are referred to as "funeral" spoons.

With the advent of silent films, a number of movie stars gained fame and spoons honoring some of these people are also collectible.

Plate 220: Engraved portrait of Pres. Wm. McKinley, gold wash, wavy handle state; Shepard; $40.00 – 65.00.

Plate 221: Pres. McKinley; Alvin; $30.00 – 50.00.

Plate 222: Pres. McKinley; also showing Mt. McKinley, the highest mountain in California; Suter; $35.00 – 60.00.

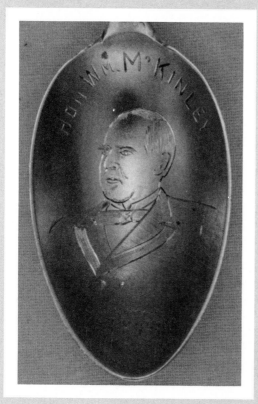

Plate 220

Plate 221

Plate 222

Plate 223: Equal Rights Amendment, Wyoming, plain bowl; unidentified manuf. mark; $40.00 – 50.00.

Plate 224: Robert Ingersol, "Liberty and Reason"; designed by Otto Wettstein; 1892; Gorham; $75.00 – 150.00.

Plate 225: Pres. Cleveland Inauguration souvenir spoon; "nominated 3 times — elected twice;" manuf. not traced; $75.00 – 120.00.

Plate 226: Robert Ingersol; no manuf. mark; $35.00 – 60.00.

Plate 223

Plate 224

Plate 225

Plate 226

Plate 227: Enamel, painted portrait of T. Roosevelt; Mechanic; $150.00 – 200.00.

Plate 228: T. Roosevelt; Mechanic; $40.00 – 60.00.

Plate 229: T. Roosevelt; Mechanic; $40.00 – 60.00.

Plate 230: President Garfield; Webb C. Bally; $40.00 – 60.00.

Plate 227

Plate 228

Plate 229

Plate 230

Plate 231: Political cartoon regarding Oklahoma statehood; Patent J.B. Bookwalter; $50.00 – 90.00.

Plate 232: Billie Possum, political satire of William Taft. The possum hides from its problems by playing dead. Wallace; $45.00 – 75.00; Billie Possum; Shiebler; $85.00 – 125.00.

Plate 233: Enameled, U.S./British friendship; Gorham H16; $100.00 – 125.00; enameled; Free Cuba; Gorham H12; $100.00 – 125.00.

Plate 234: Enameled Oklahoma "The Newest Star" (commemorative on joining the Union); state handle; Shiebler; $50.00 – 95.00.

Plate 231

Plate 233

Plate 232

Plate 234

Plate 235: The weatherman, "Fine," (a satire); enameled bowl; other versions available; J. Mayer Bros; $100.00 – 150.00.

Plate 236: Hanibal Hamlin, (Vice President under Lincoln), died 1891; $40.00 – 75.00.

Plate 237: James Blaine, (Presidential candidate, lost to Cleveland); Ryder, Krieger & Dearth mark; $40.00 – 60.00.

Plate 238: California with a "basket of bounty" finial. Engraved on the back "1933." (This is the worst time of the Great Depression and we find a sterling silver spoon touting California and indicating that it is the land of plenty. Is this a political statement?) Watson; $30.00 – 60.00.

Plate 235

Plate 236

Plate 237

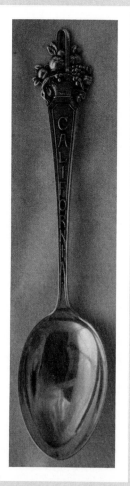

Plate 238

Plate 239: PWL (Pen Woman's League), plain bowl; Webster & Co.; $40.00 – 50.00; AAUW (American Association of University Women), plain bowl; E.J. Towle; $30.00 – 45.00.

Plate 240: WBA (Woman's Benefit Association), plain bowl; Gorham and Wood & Hughes marks; $30.00 – 50.00.

Plate 241: WCTU (Women's Christian Temperance Union); Giles Bros.; $45.00 – 75.00.

Plate 241

Plate 240

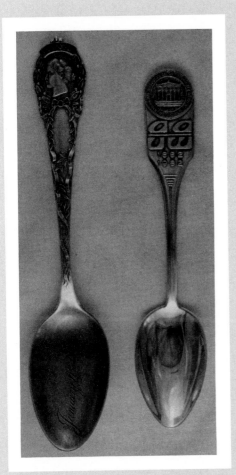

Plate 239

Plate 242: Silent movie stars, silverplated; Oneida. Left to right: Pola Negri, Norma Talmadge, Norma Shearer, Marion Davies, Lois Wilson. $8.00 – 15.00 each.

Plate 243: Silent movie stars, silverplated; Oneida. Left to right: Ramon Novarro, Thomas Meighan, Richard Dix, Douglas Fairbanks. $8.00 – 15.00 each.

Plate 242

Plate 243

Plate 244: Edwin Booth, (actor, died 1893); sold by Wanamaker; $40.00 – 60.00.

Plate 245: P.T. Barnum, "The Greatest Show on Earth," designed by Parker Davis; Shepard; $40.00 – 75.00; P.T. Barnum, dated 3/9/91; Shepard; $20.00 – 40.00.

Plate 246: Countess of Bath, New York; Gorham; $50.00 – 75.00.

Plate 247: Joseph Jefferson (1829 – 1905), (American comic actor); "Here's your good health, and your family's and may they all live long and prosper;" Howard Williamson & Sons; $50.00 – 75.00.

Plate 244

Plate 245

Plate 246

Plate 247

Plate 248: <u>Ben Hur</u>, (bestselling novel written by Lew Wallace), ca. 1880; Shepard #65; $40.00 – 75.00.

Plate 249: George Bancroft (1800 – 1891), (leading historian, <u>Complete History of the U.S.</u>), and diplomat; Durgin; $25.00 – 50.00.

Plate 250: Nathaniel Hawthorne (1804 – 1864), (leading New York author); Durgin and D. Low marks; $40.00 – 60.00.

Plate 251: Actor Fund; $80.00 – 120.00.

Plate 252: Grasshopper, Lincoln splitting logs, and locusts, (plague of the farmlands); Gorham; $150.00 – 250.00.

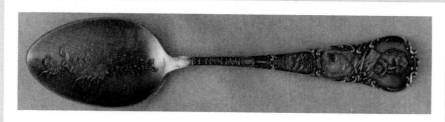

Plate 248

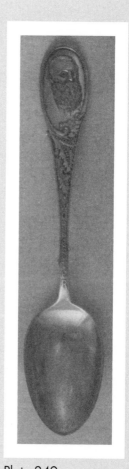

Plate 249

Plate 250

Plate 251

Plate 252

Plate 253: Watson and Newell Co. catalog, ca. 1900 – 1910.

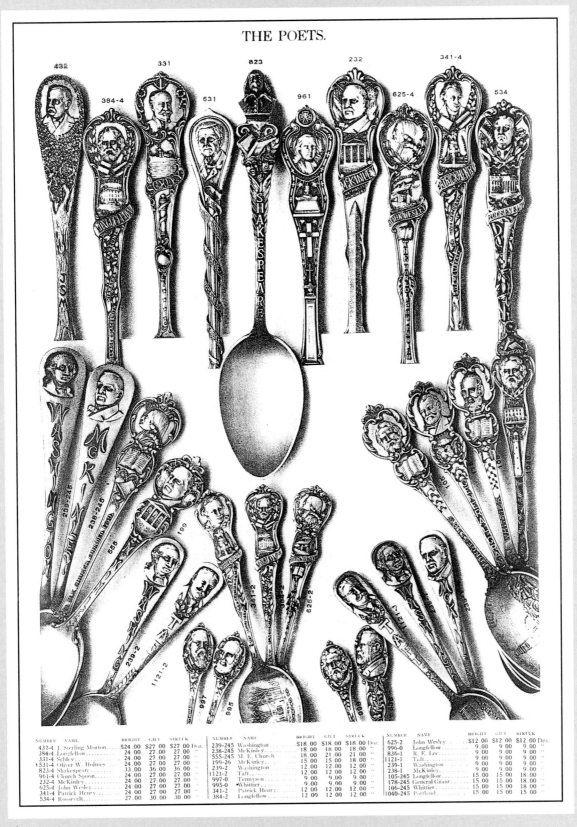

THE POETS.

NUMBER	NAME	BRIGHT	GILT	STRUCK	NUMBER	NAME	BRIGHT	GILT	STRUCK	NUMBER	NAME	BRIGHT	GILT	STRUCK
432-4	J. Sterling Morton	$24.00	$27.00	$27.00 Doz.	239-245	Washington	$18.00	$18.00	$18.00 Doz.	625-2	John Wesley	$12.00	$12.00	$12.00 Doz.
384-4	Longfellow	24.00	27.00	27.00 "	238-245	McKinley	18.00	18.00	18.00 "	996-0	Longfellow	9.00	9.00	9.00 "
331-4	Schley	24.00	27.00	27.00 "	555-245	M. E. Church	18.00	21.00	21.00 "	836-1	R. E. Lee	9.00	9.00	9.00 "
531-4	Oliver W. Holmes	24.00	27.00	27.00 "	199-26	McKinley	15.00	15.00	18.00 "	1121-1	Taft	9.00	9.00	9.00 "
823-4	Shakespeare	33.00	36.00	36.00 "	239-2	Washington	12.00	12.00	12.00 "	239-1	Washington	9.00	9.00	9.00 "
961-4	Church Spoon	24.00	27.00	27.00 "	1121-2	Taft	12.00	12.00	12.00 "	238-1	McKinley	9.00	9.00	9.00 "
232-4	McKinley	24.00	27.00	27.00 "	997-0	Tennyson	9.00	9.00	9.00 "	105-245	Longfellow	15.00	15.00	18.00 "
625-4	John Wesley	24.00	27.00	27.00 "	995-0	Whittier	9.00	9.00	9.00 "	178-245	General Grant	15.00	15.00	18.00 "
341-4	Patrick Henry	24.00	27.00	27.00 "	341-2	Patrick Henry	12.00	12.00	12.00 "	106-245	Whittier	15.00	15.00	18.00 "
534-4	Roosevelt	27.00	30.00	30.00 "	384-2	Longfellow	12.00	12.00	12.00 "	1040-245	Portland	15.00	15.00	15.00 "

Plate 253

Modern Vision of Government

Political thoughts and beliefs were fiercely debated during this time period. There were also many examples of political corruption. But generally speaking the vast majority of the populace had a strong faith in the strength, fairness, and importance of the political system. In addition there was a widespread belief that despite contemporary problems, the United States was destined to be the globe's most important country and it would soon eclipse the power of the long-established western European countries.

An unprecedented number of government buildings were built in a grand style. Capitol buildings were designed to show the power of the state. Local courthouses were the central power in the county and were built in the central square to emphasize their importance. The establishment of a post office was a major event and meant that the mighty federal government recognized the communities' importance. Public libraries were major additions to the communities' knowledge base. Government office buildings, auditoriums, etc. reflected the importance that this era placed upon established institutions. Today we take buildings of this nature with a "ho hum" attitude, but that was not the case during this dynamic period.

Most of the smaller buildings are represented by hand-engraved images in spoon bowls and the handles were either standard patterns or standard souvenir designs. The creation of embossed spoons was not economically feasible. Most examples of this genre were made in very limited editions of a dozen or less, thus they are relatively rare. At this time price does not reflect this rarity or the quality of workmanship.

Tourists frequently wanted spoons of their visits to other states and major cities. Manufacturers met this demand with an extremely wide range of styles from which to choose. State spoons were very popular and we find a tremendous variety by different manufacturers. If perchance a traveler returned home without acquiring the state-handled spoon of their choice, they could mail order them from a Sears or Montgomery Ward catalog. City spoons were also very popular. It was quite common to engrave the name of the city in the bowl of an ordinary piece of flatware or even a souvenir-handled spoon. Some collectors specialize in these areas as they produce an interesting spoon collection as well as a wide knowledge of geography.

— State Capitols —

The first and most important consideration for any state capitol building is to make a statement. In all monumental government architecture, the primary role is to show the power and the authority of the governing body. Any observer, regardless of background or education, must immediately and intuitively understand that this is a building of importance.

Both autocratic and democratic societies use the same logic, but in a democratic society, the building must also be readily accessible to the citizenry. The interior design considerations must also reflect the prevailing political philosophies. Artwork must be related to the overall theme rather than just be considered for its own beauty as in autocratic societies.

Beaux-Arts school of architecture (most of the buildings of this time period) is based upon a scholastic understanding of the power of past architectural styles. By carefully choosing certain styles, the architect reflects the prevailing political views. In most of the state capitols, for example, each of the legislative chambers is the same physical size and on the same floor so that neither can say that it is superior to the other. If the executive branch is more politically powerful, it will be on a higher floor than the legislature; if the office is to be an equal, then it will be on the same floor. The location of the supreme court within the building will also reflect its relationship to the legislative and executive offices.

The architect will pay close attention to the building materials used. Granite and marble are among the most beautiful natural materials and the most expensive. Extravagant use will be made of these materials to show the wealth and power of the state. Furthermore, the source of these materials is often of importance and careful records will be maintained as to which of the countries provided each type of building material.

Thomas Jefferson considered the dome to be the emblem of a democratic society. Most of the state capitol buildings will emulate the national capitol in Washington, D.C., and will have either central rotundas or domes over the legislative chambers. The dome will often be plated with pure gold which reflects the light and signifies to all the wealth of the state.

If possible the capitol building will be sited on a hill in the capital city. By having the building above all others, it further identifies the location of power. The appropriate choice of landscaping will accentuate the magnificence of the building.

During the late Victorian era, many new state capitol buildings were built and others were extensively remodeled to reflect the times and the new technological changes, i.e., electricity and telephones. The spoons shown here either commemorate a new or remodeled capitol building or were mementos of a citizen's visit to the state capital.

Spoons with capitol buildings impressed or engraved are very common. It would be possible to collect a capitol spoon from each of the states and this collection would have significant historical interest. Most capitol buildings also have museum-like displays and are still popular tourist attractions.

State seal spoons became very popular after the turn of the century and various styles were used by many different manufacturers. These spoons are both readily available and affordable and it would be possible to make an extensive collection. They are also quite interesting because of the many popular attractions featured on both the front and back.

Plate 254: Detail of bowl in Plate 255.

Plate 255: Cannon; $50.00 – 120.00.

Plate 254

Plate 255

Plate 256: Enameled, Oregon finial; $20.00 – 40.00.

Plate 257: Detail, four embossed views of Denver Capitol Building; see complete spoons in other chapters; note the wide variety of perspective on the same building

Plate 258: Postcard.

Plate 257

Plate 256

Plate 258

Plate 259: Washington Monument, pat. 11/18/90; $40.00 – 60.00.

Plate 260: Engraved, Madison, Wisconsin; Old English pattern; Towle; $25.00 – 50.00.

Plate 261: Wavy handle state spoon; an obvious knockoff of the Shepard series; Deacon; $15.00 – 30.00.

Plate 259

Plate 260

Plate 261

Plate 262: State Series; other states available; J. Meyer Bros.; $15.00 – 30.00 each.

Plate 263: Wavy handled state spoons; these are found with plain bowls, gilt bowls, embossed bowls; engraved pictures or names, enamel pictures, etc.; Shepard; $15.00 – 30.00 each.

Plate 264: State Series; other states available; Gorham; $15.00 – 30.00 each.

Plate 262

Plate 263

Plate 264

Plate 265: State spoons; other states in this series available; Ohio, Fessenden Company; Colorado, Deacon; South Dakota, Wallace. $15.00 – 30.00 each.

Plate 266: States, other similar states available; Montana, gold washed serving bowl; Wm. Linker; $25.00 – 50.00; Oregon, engraved webfoot in bowl; Mechanic; $25.00 – 50.00.

Plate 265

Plate 266

Plate 267: State Series; Manchester/Baker; other states available; $15.00 – 30.00 each.

Plate 268: State Series; Mechanic; other states available; $15.00 – 30.00 each.

Plate 267

Plate 268

Plate 269: State Series; Watson; other states available; $15.00 – 30.00 each.

Plate 270: State Series; Paye & Baker; other states available; $15.00 – 30.00 each.

Plate 269

Plate 270

Plate 271: State handle; embossed bowl; Denver capitol; ELD; $15.00 – 25.00.

Plate 272: States, other states with similar handles available; Ohio, R. Lunt; $25.00 – 40.00; Arizona, Grand Canyon, Robbins; $15.00 – 30.00; Georgia, Manchester/Baker; $15.00 – 30.00.

Plate 273: States; American Collectors Guild; silver-plated; $2.00 – 5.00.

Plate 271

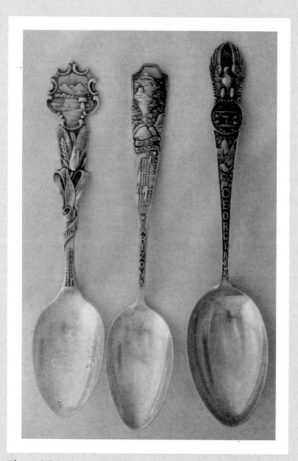

Plate 272

Plate 273

Plate 274: States. Alaska, demi, transfer print enamel finial; sterling; (also made in base metal); Klepa Arts, Holland; $5.00 – 15.00; New York, demi; Alvin; $5.00 – 15.00; Oregon, demi; no manuf. mark; $5.00 – 15.00; Colorado, demi; untraced manuf.; $5.00 – 15.00.

Plate 274

Plate 275: Watson and Newell Co. catalog, ca. 1900 – 1910.

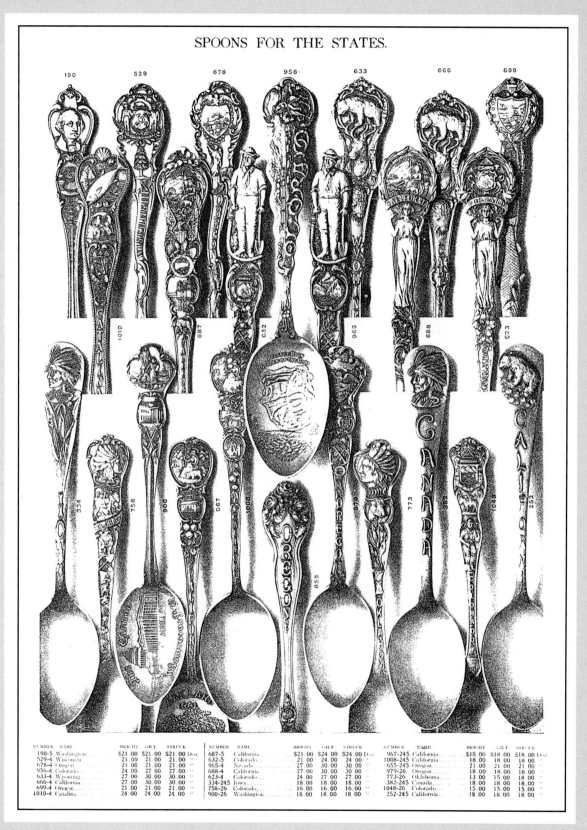

Plate 275

— Cities —

City hall architecture tended to follow the current prevalent styles. Many city halls were enlarged during this time period because cities generally were providing more services to the citizenry than in the past. The increased size was necessary to house the increase in city employees and to remodel the buildings to accommodate new technological improvements.

Typically a city hall would not be an attraction for tourists. When we find spoons engraved with a picture of the city hall, it is usually a commemorative from the opening ceremonies. These spoons are fairly rare and it would be very difficult to find any one city in particular.

Plate 276: Crescent City, Mardi Gras, New Orleans; Paye & Baker; $40.00 – 75.00.

Plate 277: "Seeing" series, Mechanics; Chicago; Washington, D.C.; St. Louis; $125.00 – 175.00 each.

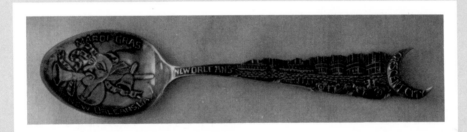

Plate 276

Plate 277

Plate 278: Engraved, City Hall, St. Louis, Missouri; Shepard; $35.00 – 50.00.

Plate 279: Los Angeles, City of Angels, ca. 1904; $40.00 – 75.00. Los Angeles, San Gabriel Mission; $30.00 – 50.00.

Plate 280: Boston; $25.00 – 45.00; Bangor, Maine; Gorham; $30.00 – 50.00; Buffalo, New York; Shiebler; $30.00 – 60.00.

Plate 278

Plate 279

Plate 280

Plate 281: Engraved, residence scene, Portland, Oregon; Meyer Bros; $30.00 – 50.00.

Plate 282: Engraved, City Hall; Elgin, Illinois; Shepard; $35.00 – 50.00.

Plate 283: New Orleans, Mardi Gras, painted bowl; $45.00 – 70.00.

Plate 281

Plate 282

Plate 283

Plate 284: Bon bon spoons; $50.00 – 125.00.

Plate 285: Engraved, City Hall, South Bend, Indiana; Buttercup pattern; Gorham; $35.00 – 50.00

Plate 286: Pasadena, Calif., (home of the New Year's Day Rose Parade); Rebus spoon "Crown of the Valley;" Mechanics; $40.00 – 75.00.

Plate 284

Plate 285

Plate 286

Plate 287: Civic booster, figural lady, enameled bowl and finial, Spokane; no manuf. mark; $100.00 – 150.00; San Diego, enameled bowl (transfer print), Ramona's wedding place; $40.00 – 60.00.

Plate 288: Intertwined city names. Many variations available. Chicago, Manchester/Baker; $20.00 – 40.00; Saratoga; Durgin; $20.00 – 35.00.

Plate 289: Buffalo, New York; Durgin (designed T.V. Dickenson); $30.00 – 45.00.

Plate 287

Plate 288

Plate 289

Plate 290: Engraved, webfoot; State series; Portland, Oregon; play on the amount of rain; Mechanics; $40.00 – 60.00.

Plate 291: Cut-out city names, from the 1920s, plain bowls; $15.00 – 30.00 each; Milwaukee, marked "82;" Earlham, Whiting; Kansas City, Paye & Baker; Utica, Whiting; Sioux City, Watson; Hot Springs, Robbins; Hartland, Manchester/Baker; Hanford, Meyer Bros; Moline, Whiting; machine pounded handle, dated "22."

Plate 290

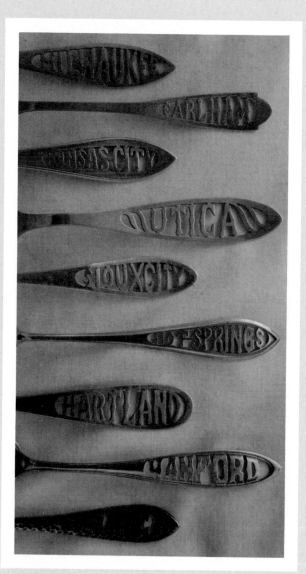

Plate 291

Plate 292: Watson and Newell Co. catalog, ca. 1900 – 1910.

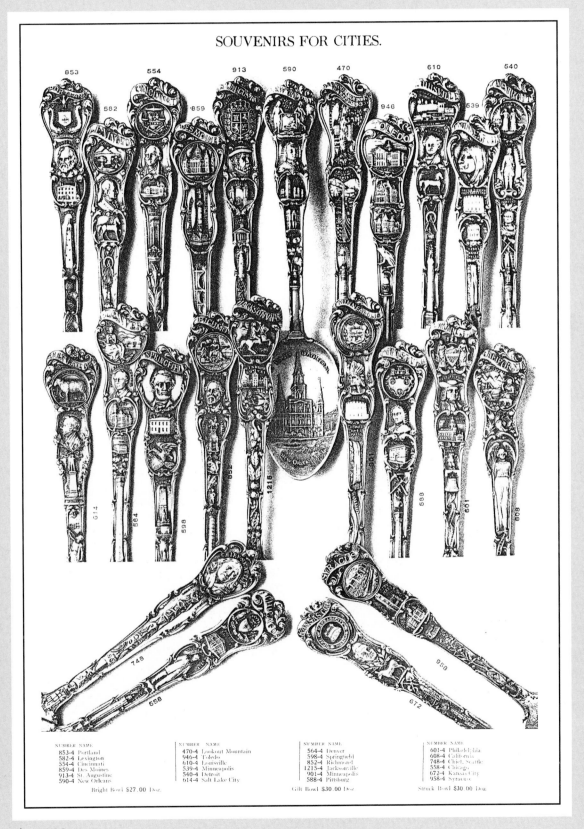

Plate 292

— Courthouses —

The courthouse was a grand symbol of the importance of the county and the town. In this era it was deemed important to convert the abstract concepts of "Democracy and the Law" into tangible real property, and architects labored incessantly to make the architecture of the building reflect the civilizing influence of the law. Public buildings were required to show the awesome majesty of government and were further designed to make the individual feel both insignificant as a mere mortal and inspired by the greatness of historical tradition.

The building would normally be sited in a landscaped square in the middle of town and monuments would be erected in the park-like area. In some towns streets would be numbered from the central square.

Courthouses were mainly of significance to the local community and spoons showing these edifices were often commemoratives of the opening ceremonies which were often very extensive. Most of the spoons have bright-cut hand-engraved pictures of the building and were commissioned by local jewelers in very limited editions (usually 12 or less). Many of the courthouses have been remodeled, thus these sterling silver mementos are one of the few records of their original glory.

Courthouse spoons are moderately rare and it would be very difficult to find a particular courthouse spoon. A general collector of these beautifully engraved spoons, however, can develop a fine collection with great historical interest.

Plate 293: Engraved, Fort Wayne, Indiana; wavy handle; Shepard; $40.00 – 60.00.

Plate 294: Engraved, Pittsfield, Illinois; Whiting; $30.00 – 50.00.

Plate 293

Plate 294

Plate 295: Engraved, Tipton, Indiana; $30.00 – 50.00.

Plate 296: Engraved, Rock Island; Illinois; Watson; $30.00 – 50.00.

Plate 297: Stalking Indian with corn; engraved Spokane, Washington courthouse; SSMC; $40.00 – 80.00.

Plate 298: Engraved, Fresno, California; Art Nouveau nude; Watson; $50.00 – 80.00.

Plate 295

Plate 297

Plate 296

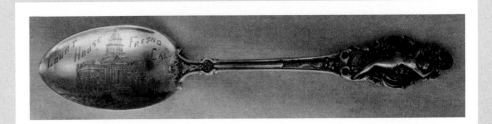

Plate 298

Plate 299: Engraved, Findlay, Ohio; corn design; SSMC; $50.00 – 75.00.

Plate 300: Engraved, Allegan, Michigan; Old Newbury pattern, ca. 1900; Towle; $30.00 – 50.00.

Plate 301: Engraved, Troy, Ohio; Shepard; $30.00 – 50.00.

Plate 299

Plate 300

Plate 301

Plate 302: Engraved, Rochester, Indiana; bright-cut flower pattern; Paye & Baker; $30.00 – 55.00.

Plate 303: Engraved, Virginia, Illinois; Irving pattern; Wallace; $30.00 – 50.00.

Plate 304: Engraved, Hebron, Nebraska; La Viola pattern; Wallace; $30.00 – 50.00.

Plate 302

Plate 303

Plate 304

Plate 305: Engraved, Shreveport, Louisiana; SSMC; $30.00 – 50.00.

Plate 306: Engraved, Marietta, Ohio; Irving pattern; Wallace; $30.00 – 50.00.

Plate 307: Engraved, Ravenna, Ohio; Old Newbury Pattern, ca. 1900; Towle; $30.00 – 50.00.

Plate 305

Plate 306

Plate 307

— Libraries —

The concept of the library stretches back into history for thousands of years. But the free public library system which we enjoy in the United States is a fairly recent development. Prior to the 1880s there were very few such libraries. Most of the existing libraries were privately owned or operated by subscription, i.e., those who contributed books could use the library. Andrew Carnegie was a poor boy who made a huge amount of money by building the largest steel company in the world. After he retired, he created several foundations. One of these was to build local libraries which would be available to everyone, regardless of assets. The story is that he was a voracious reader and had obtained the privilege of using a subscription library. But when he was a teen, that library had budget problems and he was denied access because of his inability to pay. He vowed that when he became wealthy, no one would be denied access to knowledge because they were poor.

The Carnegie Foundation made contracts with over 1,600 communities wherein it would provide the money to build a free-standing library building and the community would agree to buy books, hire librarians, and provide continuing expenses. It is mainly because of Carnegie's money and initiative that this country now enjoys one of the best free public library systems in the world. This book could not have been written without the cooperation of several public libraries.

Library spoons are moderately rare. It would be very difficult to find a specific library, but it is possible to develop a collection of library spoons.

Plate 308: Engraved, Blackstone Public Library; Lancaster pattern, ca. 1897; Gorham; $30.00 – 50.00.

Plate 308

Plate 309: Engraved, Public Library, Marseilles, Illinois; state handle; Paye & Baker; $40.00 – 60.00.

Plate 310: Engraved, Musser Public Library, Muscatine, Iowa; Cambridge pattern, ca. 1899; Gorham; $30.00 – 50.00.

Plate 311: Engraved, Carnegie Library, Rockford, Illinois; Chantilly pattern, ca. 1895; Gorham; $30.00 – 50.00.

Plate 309

Plate 310

Plate 311

Plate 312: Engraved, Carnegie Library, Chanute, Kansas; Manchester/Baker; $30.00 – 50.00.

Plate 313: Engraved, library, Toledo, Ohio; Majestic pattern, ca. 1900; Alvin; $30.00 – 50.00.

Plate 314: Engraved, library, Pomona, California; Shepard; $30.00 – 50.00.

Plate 312

Plate 313

Plate 314

Plate 315: Engraved, Carnegie Benington library, Winterset, Iowa; unident. manuf.; $30.00 – 50.00.

Plate 316: Engraved, Public Library, Minneapolis, Minnesota; Fessenden; $30.00 – 50.00.

Plate 315

Plate 316

— Post Offices —

The major method of communication between people in different geographic areas was the postal system. The telegraph was faster, but it was very expensive to use. The telephone had been demonstrated, but its full potential would not be apparent for several decades. By 1901 there were 76,945 post offices in the U.S. The establishment of a local post office in most cities and towns was an event of immense local significance because it meant that the town had arrived and the community would celebrate the opening by staging a parade with the local school band playing their instruments and dignitaries making profound speeches. It tied the community into the postal service's "world wide web." In anticipation of these ceremonies, the local jeweler would often arrange for a few spoons to be hand engraved with a view of the new building. Because of the significant cost, relatively few spoons were made for each event (usually 12 or less), but there were a lot of events. Thus each commemorative spoon is relatively rare, but it is still possible to find nice post office commemorative spoons. Most of these buildings have been demolished and many of the spoons have been melted during the last century, thus these remaining commemorative souvenirs are one of the few records of their existence.

Post office spoons are moderately rare.

Plate 317: Engraved, new post office, Kansas City, Missouri; Paye & Baker; $40.00 – 60.00.

Plate 318: Engraved, post office, Kansas City; Missouri (alternate view); $30.00 – 50.00.

Plate 317

Plate 318

Plate 319: Engraved, post office, Williamsport, Pennsylvania; Louis XV, ca. 1891; Whiting; $30.00 – 50.00.

Plate 320: Engraved, new post office, Houston, Texas; SSMC; $40.00 – 60.00.

Plate 321: Engraved, post office, Scranton, Pennsylvania; Manchester/Baker; $30.00 – 50.00.

Plate 319

Plate 320

Plate 321

Plate 322: Engraved, post office, Indianapolis, Indiana; Fessenden; $30.00 – 50.00.

Plate 323: Engraved, post office, Kokomo, Indiana; John Hancock pattern, ca. 1911; Lunt; $30.00 – 50.00.

Plate 324: Engraved, post office, Jacksonville, Florida; bright-cut flower handle; $40.00 – 60.00.

Plate 322

Plate 324

Plate 323

— Other Government Buildings —

Plate 325: Engraved, state reformatory, Pontiac, Michigan; Alvin, fleur-de-lis pattern, ca. 1907; $40.00 – 80.00.

Plate 326: Engraved, state penetenionary (sic), Rawlings, Wyoming; Watson; $40.00 – 80.00.

Plate 325

Plate 326

Plate 327: Engraved, state prison, Waupin, Wisconsin; Puritan pattern, ca. 1910; Wallace; $40.00 – 80.00.

Plate 328: Engraved, Memorial Hall, Lima, Ohio; Whiting; $30.00 – 50.00.

Plate 329: Rock Island, Illinois Arsenal, plain bowl; J. Ramser; $15.00 – 25.00.

Plate 327

Plate 328

Plate 329

Plate 330: Engraved, U.S. Mint; Denver, Colorado; Manchester/Baker; $30.00 – 50.00.

Plate 331: Postcard, United States Mint, Denver, Colorado.

Plate 332: Standing Indian finial, engraved auditorium, Vinita, Oklahoma; Paye & Baker; $35.00 – 75.00.

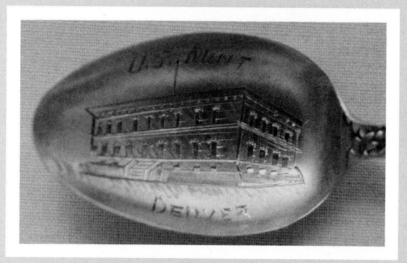

Plate 330

Plate 332

Plate 331

Plate 333: Fish finial, engraved auditorium, Long Beach, California; dated 1894; Mechanic; $35.00 – 80.00.

Plate 334: Engraved, auditorium, Omaha, Nebraska; Weidlich; $30.00 – 50.00.

Plate 335: Engraved, government building, Jacksonville, Florida; Shepard; $30.00 – 50.00.

Plate 334

Plate 333

Plate 335

Miracles of Technology

During the 1885 – 1920 time period, the United States was undergoing a technological revolution unprecedented in the history of the world. Giant business corporations and trusts completely altered the business environment. New steel technology was radically affecting the shapes of buildings and the city with dramatic changes to life styles, customs, and traditions. Energy generation would soon influence homes' interiors, the workplace, and modes of transportation. The development of the telephone would soon redefine the very nature of communication and interpersonal relationships. The development of motor- and electric-powered transportation would further redesign the urban landscape and affect the nature of both work and leisure. New scientific developments changed the way people viewed the cosmos, religion, and their own personal lives. Other technological advances began to make obsolete traditional skills and redirect the future of virtually every citizen. Even greater change from new technologies such as the airplane and the automobile promised even more fantastic events in the next decades. The radical advances would affect people and the culture in unprecedented ways .

— Skylines and Skyscrapers —

New building materials and new technical concepts were combined during this time period in innovative ways which would dramatically influenced the city, people's lives, and the entire twentieth century.

The greatest American innovation in architecture was the skyscraper. Previously, buildings were limited in size to the strength of the wall materials. The weight of the upper stories was conducted through the load-bearing walls to the ground. Using existing technology, a maximum height of about 60 feet could be obtained. Beyond that height the walls could not withstand the force of gravity.

The improvement in steel quality created a material which could support substantially more weight. In addition the development of the cantilevered system (the architectural equivalent of the development of the wheel) allowed builders to construct higher, stronger buildings than ever before. Chicago was the leading city for the development of these huge buildings. In 1885 the first building to reach a "staggering" height of 10 stories was constructed. This breathtaking building was built by William Jenney who developed a steel metal framework which supported the roof, floors, and walls. The exterior walls were literally hung on the steel beams much as we hang curtains on a rod while the steel infrastructure supported all the weight. The exteriors of buildings could now contain significant amounts of non-weight bearing materials, such as glass, which would permanently change the way buildings looked.

The future of the central city would continue upward. New skyscrapers were soon built in all the major cities and many of them would be commemorated on sterling silver spoons. In New York the Singer Building and the Flatiron Building became major contributors to the new skyline and very popular symbols on spoons. In 1916 the giant Woolworth Building would redefine skyscraper architecture with its massive Gothic tower piercing the heavens. These new buildings significantly added to the prestige of the United States and changed the very complexions of the cities. The new commercial superstructures would now dominate the skyline and dwarf all existing buildings.

Souvenir skyline spoons are still very popular and desirable collectibles.

Plate 336: Seattle; Paye & Baker; $50.00 – 90.00; Detroit; Paye & Baker; $50.00 – 90.00; Detroit; Paye & Baker; $50.00 – 90.00.

Plate 337: Reverse of Plate 336.

Plate 336

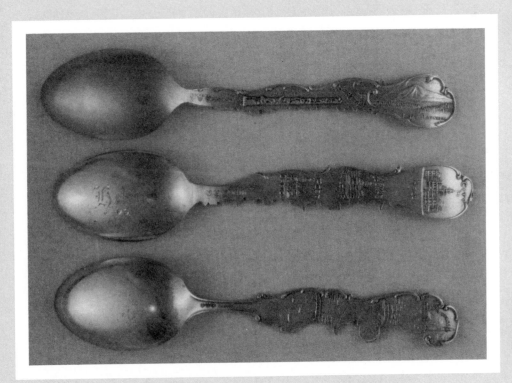

Plate 337

Plate 338: Chicago; Paye & Baker; $40.00 – 80.00; Pittsburgh; Paye & Baker; $50.00 – 90.00; Baltimore; Paye & Baker; $70.00 – 100.00.

Plate 339: New York; Mechanic; $40.00 – 80.00; New York; Metropolitan Life Building; $40.00 – 80.00; Duluth, Minnesota; J.B.E. registered; $50.00 – 90.00.

Plate 338

Plate 339

Plate 340: Chicago, Grant Monument; Mechanic; $50.00 – 80.00.

Plate 341: Enclosed skylines (post World War I). Fork, North Yakima, Washington, showing high school, Masonic temple and courthouse; SSMC; $30.00 – 50.00; Salt Lake City, Utah, showing The Tabernacle, courthouse, state capitol, and temple; no manuf. mark; $ 20.00 – 40.00; Salina, Kansas, KW business, Sacred Heart School, Wesleyan University, St. John's Military School, high school; Robbins; $20.00 – 40.00; New Orleans, Louisiana, showing Canal Street; Watson; $20.00 – 40.00.

Plate 340

Plate 341

Plate 342: Engraved, Woolworth Building, New York; $35.00 – 75.00 depending on handle.

Plate 343: New York; Paye & Baker; $40.00 – 70.00; Cleveland; Paye & Baker; $50.00 – 90.00; New York; Paye & Baker; $40.00 – 70.00.

Plate 342

Plate 343

Plate 344: Memphis; Shepard; $70.00 – 90.00.

Plate 345: Embossed, Flatiron Building, New York; $20.00 – 75.00 depending on handle.

Plate 346: Postcard, Flatiron Building.

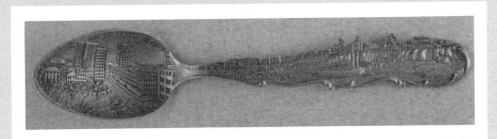

Plate 344

Plate 345

Plate 346

Plate 347: Pittsburgh; Paye & Baker; $50.00 – 85.00.

Plate 348: Engraved, Singer Building, New York; Hamilton pattern; Alvin; $30.00 – 50.00.

Plate 349: Engraved, Wells Building, Milwaukee; Strousberg pattern; Gorham; $30.00 – 50.00.

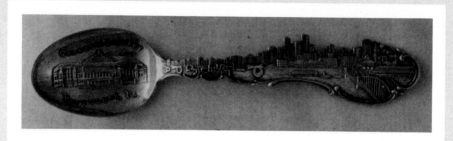

Plate 347

Plate 348

Plate 349

— Energy Resources —

The development of new energy sources had an immense impact on the twentieth century. Black gold (oil) was first used to improve lighting and allow people to work at night. Later it was used as the basis for gasoline which would power hundreds of millions of automobiles. These automobiles had a profound effect on people all over the globe and would alter virtually every aspect of our civilization in many unforeseen ways. The finding of a new oil field was a financial bonanza and made many "instant" millionaires. It was only natural to commemorate such good fortune by having silver spoons engraved with a picture of the new source of wealth. These spoons are fairly rare and are desireable collectibles. Some generic spoons depicting oil wells demonstrate that tourists would often visit oil fields.

The development of new hydro-electric plants enabled the community to have a cheap source of electrical energy. Electricity would soon become a basic in every house and office in the land and change lives in thousands of ways. New hydro-electric projects were expensive for local communities to build and their opening was often commemorated in sterling silver. Unfortunately dams and water projects often are not pictorially pretty so the bowls of these spoons are not dramatic, but their significance outweighs artistic efforts.

Plate 350: Engraved dams and hydroelectric projects; various manuf.; $30.00 – 50.00 each.

Plate 350

Plate 351: Engraved, Coon River Dam, Iowa; Virginia pattern; Lunt; $40.00 – 60.00.

Plate 352: Engraved, shooting oil well, Alexandria, Indiana; prob. commem.; Shepard; $50.00 – 75.00.

Plate 353: Engraved, gusher oil well, Sapulpa, Oklahoma; pat. 1898; prob. commem.; Towle; $50.00 – 70.00.

Plate 351

Plate 352

Plate 353

Note: We have two types of oil well spoons. First are the spoons which were designed to commemorate a specific oil find. Second are spoons designed to be sold to visitors to an oil-producing area. These are sometimes generic with a space available for customizing.

Plate 354: Engraved, water works, Morrison, Illinois; Stuart pattern; Towle; $30.00 – 50.00.

Plate 355: Engraved, gusher oil well, prob. commemorative of an oil strike; Towle, ca. 1898; $50.00 – 75.00.

Plate 356: Engraved, oil derrick, Lima, Ohio; Watson; $50.00 – 70.00.

Plate 354

Plate 355

Plate 356

Plate 357: Flowing oil well, generic acid etched bowl designed with a space for engraved customizing; Revere pattern, ca. 1898; Wilcox and Evertson; $20.00 – 30.00.

Plate 358: Engraved oil field, Bradford, Pennyslvania; Watson; $40.00 – 70.00.

Plate 359: Engraved oil wells, Bolivar, N.Y.; bright-cut handle; unidentified manuf.; $50.00 – 80.00.

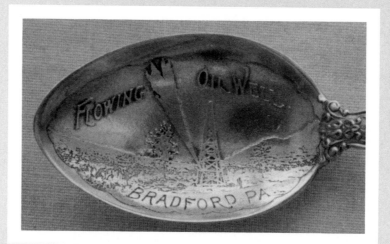

Plate 357

Plate 358

Plate 359

Plate 360: Marseilles Dam, Illinois state handle; Paye & Baker; $30.00 – 45.00.

Plate 361: Engraved commem. oil gusher (Jan. 10, 1903); Bakersfield, Calif.; no manuf. mark. $50.00 – 80.00.

Plate 362: Engraved oil well, Chanute, Kansas; Manchester/Baker; $50.00 – 70.00.

Plate 360

Plate 361

Plate 362

— Transportation and Bridges —

One of the more dramatic changes that occurred during 1890 – 1920 was the development of new transportation. Until the 1870s land transportation of people and goods was basically limited to human power (walking) or animal power (wagons, stage coaches, etc.). The development of the railroad radically changed the speed, expense, and ease of travel over longer distances. The completion of thousands of rail lines linked the Eastern and Western coasts and thousands of points in between. Within the city, the development of electric and cable trolleys greatly affected the size and development of urban communities. In the early 1890s human powered bicycles were a huge fad and they began to change local transportation and the women's role in society, i.e., job locations, styles of dress, etc. In the late 1890s self-propelled cars started to appear on local streets and the automobile would eventually become one of the most significant factors influencing the size and look of urban areas since the dawn of time. At this time preliminary attempts would be made to enable men to fly, and in 1903 the Wright brothers made the first sustained powered flight. In the decades after the turn of the century, the automobile and airplane would affect every city and every individual in multiple profound ways.

Automobiles require paved roads for optimum performance. Massive road building projects were undertaken in all parts of the country. Oftentimes geography created problems. New technology encouraged road builders to drill holes through mountains, creating tunnels.

Of even more significance, the new developments in steel production combined with innovative concepts would greatly expand the role of the bridge in linking communities separated by the sea, rivers or other narrow waterways. The Eads Bridge in St. Louis was a pioneering effort in the application of this new technology and it is celebrated on many spoons. Perhaps of even greater significance is the Brooklyn Bridge which used daring new suspension technology combined with innovative artistic and structural designs. Besides being a monument to man's ability to span large ocean waterways in an urban setting, it created the opportunity to link New York City to Brooklyn, creating one of the world's greatest metropolises. The significance of this bridge was far-reaching and has had an impact on virtually every major city in the world. "The air-bridged harbor that twin-cities frame" in the Lazarus poem in Chapter 1 is a reference to this bridge. Several hundred varieties of Brooklyn Bridge spoons have been identified.

In addition to these major engineering feats, we frequently find smaller bridges on spoons because the local residents realized their great importance to the local community. Almost all of the local bridge spoons were commemorative of their grand openings.

Plate 363: Crescent City, New Orleans; Paye & Baker; $40.00 – 80.00.

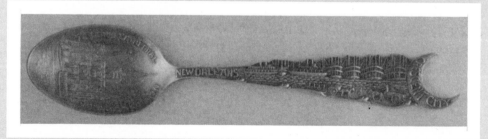

Plate 363

Plate 364: De Witt Clinton steam engine, enameled, engraved train; Schenectady, N.Y.; Shepard #55; $75.00 – 140.00.

Plate 365: Engraved, lighthouse, Harbor Point, Mich.; Provence pattern; Fessenden; $40.00 – 60.00.

Plate 366: Delta Line; no manuf. mark; $35.00 – 70.00; passenger ship, Watson, ca. 1915; $25.00 – 50.00.

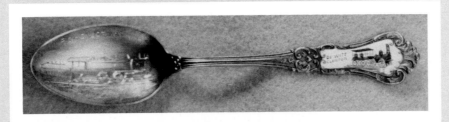

Plate 364

Plate 365

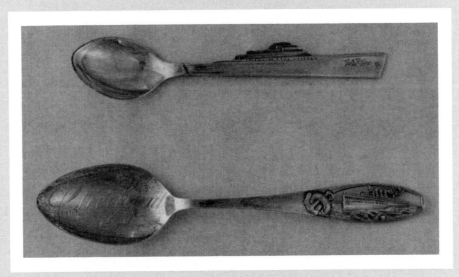

Plate 366

Plate 367: Train, Diablo Canyon, Arizona, A.T.&S.F.; Mechanics; $75.00 – 125.00; train, manuf. for Fred Harvey souvenir shop; Mechanics; $50.00 – 125.00; train, acid etched bowl, Memphis; Mechanics; $50.00 – 85.00.

Plate 368: Reverse of Diablo Canyon Train.

Plate 367

Plate 368

Plate 369: Engraved train, Renovo, Pa., Shepard; $30.00 – 50.00.

Plate 370: Burlington Train Station, Omaha, Nebraska; Shepard, #2 pattern; $30.00 – 60.00.

Plate 371: Altoona, Pa., train and embossed horseshoe bend; W.E. Sellers & Co.; $40.00 – 60.00.

Plate 369

Plate 370

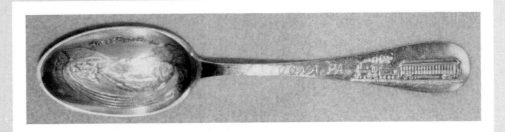

Plate 371

Plate 372: Detail, biking phenomenon; no manuf. mark; $30.00 – 75.00.

Plate 373: Mt. Penn and Neversink RR; Reading, Pa.; Durgin (designed by C.A. Schlechter); $50.00 – 80.00.

Plate 374: Haynes Light Six automobile; Paye & Baker; $60.00 – 90.00.

Plate 372

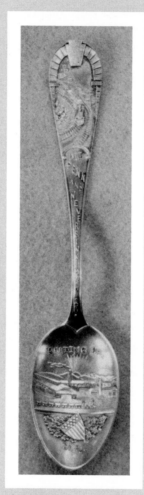

Plate 373

Plate 374

Plate 375: Wright Brothers; $25.00 – 40.00.

Plate 376: Engraved, Port Huron; unidentified pattern, ca. 1899; Gorham; $30.00 – 50.00.

Plate 377: Engraved, launching scene, Newport News; Shepard; $30.00 – 50.00.

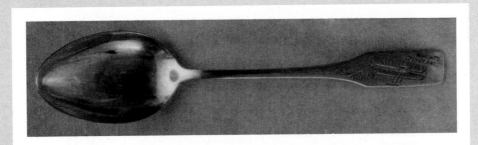

Plate 375

Plate 376

Plate 377

Plate 378: Train, copper insert on silver and engraved; J. Mayer Bros.; $40.00 – 90.00.

Plate 379: Engraved, Union Station, St. Louis; Black Starr; $30.00 – 50.00.

Plate 380: Engraved, Duluth; Buttercup pattern; Gorham; $30.00 – 50.00.

Plate 378

Plate 379

Plate 380

Plate 381: Engraved, Union Depot, Troy, New York; unidentified manuf.; $30.00 – 50.00.

Plate 382: Embossed, General Engine; no maker mark; $15.00 – 25.00.

Plate 383: "Ashtabula Disaster," Dec. 29, 1876; enamel finial. Shepard. (This is a commemorative spoon for either the 20th or 25th anniversary of the disaster.) $175.00 – 250.00.

Plate 384: Detail of Plate 383, embossed.

Plate 381

Plate 382

Plate 383

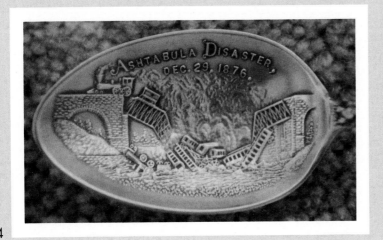

Plate 384

Plate 385: Engraved, Spiral Bridge; Hastings, Minnesota; Gorham; $50.00 – 70.00.

Plate 386: Engraved, Main St. Bridge, Crookston, Minnesota; Paye & Baker; $30.00 – 50.00.

Plate 387: Engraved, "new million dollar bridge," Toledo, Ohio; (prob. souvenir of grand opening); Hamilton pattern; Alvin; $50.00 – 75.00.

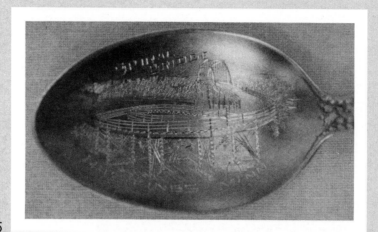

Plate 385

Plate 386

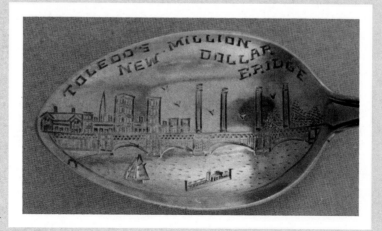

Plate 387

Plate 388: Engraved, suspension bridge, Cincinnati, Ohio; Floral Lily pattern; Whiting; $25.00 – 40.00.

Plate 389: Engraved, aerial bridge, Duluth, Minnesota; (fairly common with many variations); Shepard; $25.00 – 200.00.

Plate 390: Engraved, covered bridge (rare), Cambridge, Ohio; Windsor pattern, ca. 1890; Wallace; $35.00 – 60.00.

Plate 388

Plate 389

Plate 390

Plate 391: Engraved bridges; various manuf.; $30.00 – 75.00 each.

Plate 391

Plate 392: Engraved, Brooklyn Bridge; Simpson; $35.00 – 70.00; Waverly pattern, ca. 1892; Wallace; $35.00 – 70.00.

Plate 393: Cincinnati Bridge; Paye & Baker; $50.00 – 75.00; Duluth Bridge; unidentified maker; $30.00 – 60.00.

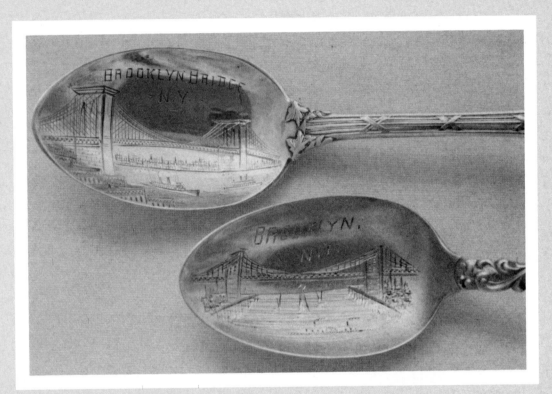

Plate 392

Plate 393

Plate 394: Brooklyn Bridge, Stuyvesant; Shepard; $50.00 – 70.00.

Plate 395: Engraved, high bridge; Iowa Rapids; Iowa; Mothers pattern; Gorham; $30.00 – 50.00.

Plate 396: Engraved, bridge, Selma, Alabama; Shepard; $30.00 – 50.00.

Plate 394

Plate 395

Plate 396

Plate 397: Engraved, Duluth Bridge, enameled crossed rifles; $150.00 – 200.00.

Plate 398: Eads Bridge, St. Louis, Missouri; $20.00 – 40.00.

Plate 399: Engraved, Port Huron train tunnel; unidentified pattern; Gorham; $25.00 – 40.00.

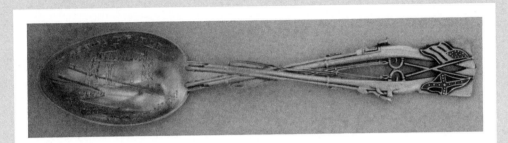

Plate 397

Plate 398

Plate 399

— Health and Medicine —

Being healthy was always of major concern to both the individual and the community. The last decades of the nineteenth century produced new medical breakthroughs and scientific evidence to show the importance of sanitary conditions. The building of a local hospital was of great importance and a natural subject for a spoon.

Sanitariums were places for the wealthy to unwind and relax in luxury. Many spoons have a rich historical background that is not evident on the surface. One such example is the Battle Creek Sanitarium. The director was Dr. Kellogg who believed in a very natural diet and developed a number of recipes which would make this roughage palatable to human taste. One of the frequent visitors to this sanitarium was Mr. Post. He thought these recipes would be a market success and Dr. Kellogg obliged by giving him several of these secret formulas. The Post Breakfast Cereal Company was an instant hit. Dr. Kellogg, seeing the commercial possiblilities, established his own company to make breakfast cereal. Battle Creek, Michigan, is still the world's largest supplier of breakfast cereals. Many other spoons have similar historical importance and only require research.

Plate 400: Engraved, State Hospital, Massillon, Ohio; Shepard; $30.00 – 50.00; engraved, City Hospital, Watertown, N.Y.; Rose pattern, Wallace; $30.00 – 50.00.

Plate 401: Dr. G.W. Leille; "Dedicated to my patients who have survived my practice;" (note pill in the bowl); Mechanics; $100.00 – 300.00.

Plate 400

Plate 401

154

Plate 402: Engraved, State Insane Asylum, Nevada, Missouri; Shepard; $40.00 – 70.00.

Plate 403: Battle Creek Sanitarium, Battle Creek, Mich.; (building was rebuilt after being destroyed by fire); Shepard; $30.00 – 50.00; wavy handle; Shepard; $40.00 – 60.00.

Plate 402

Plate 403

Plate 404: Dr. F.E. Townsend; silver-plated; Shepard; $5.00 – 15.00.

Plate 405: Engraved, St. Mary's Hospital, Rochester, Minn; Alvin, $30.00 – 50.00; engraved, hospital, Batavia, N.Y.; NS Co., $30.00 – 50.00.

Plate 406: Engraved, St. Joseph Sanitarium, Mt. Clemens, Mich.; (building was rebuilt after being destroyed by fire); unidentified manuf. $30.00 – 50.00; Lansterling pattern; Gorham; $30.00 – 50.00.

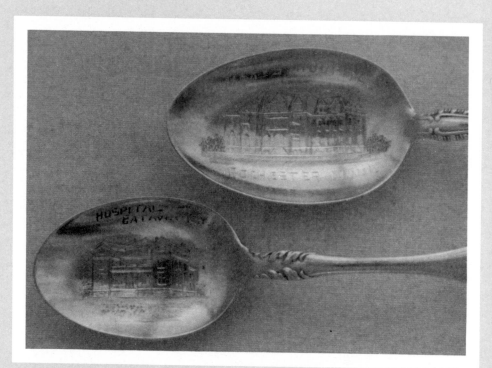

Plate 405

Plate 404

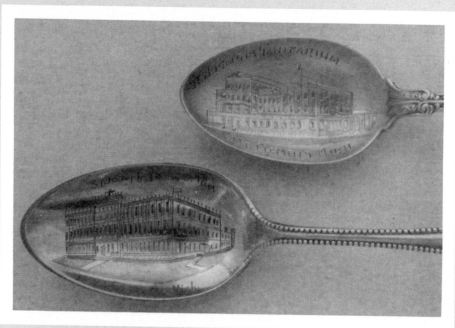

Plate 406

— Industry and Business —

The era of the souvenir spoon movement coincided with the growth of the largest business conglomerates heretofore known. Names such as Carnegie, Rockefeller, and Morgan dominated their industries, but there were also many other consolidations in smaller industries. In silver manufacturing, for example, numerous smaller manufactories joined forces under the name International Silver. These huge conglomerates would influence the shape of business for the next hundred years.

Factories were large buildings and employed many workers. In many communities they were a major component of the economic health of the town. Sterling spoons referring to a specific factory are fairly rare. They may have been made as commemoratives for the top executives or they may have been used as sophisticated advertising tools to major clients. Silver-plated spoons were often advertising vehicles (also see advertising spoons). Spoons referring to an "industrial area" were often made for tourists.

Plate 407: Commercial Travelers Insurance Company, (failed attempt at affinity sales); salesman with briefcase; no manuf. mark; $75.00 – 125.00; Mercury on globe; Niagara Silver Co.; $75.00 – 125.00; Commercial Travelers Home Office; no manuf. mark; Mason advertising; $75.00 – 90.00.

Plate 408: Engraved, Junction Bldg., Kansas City, Mo.; Watson; $20.00 – 30.00; (note the poor quality of the engraving and artistry).

Plate 407

Plate 408

Plate 409: Milling district; Minneapolis, Minnesota; Paye & Baker; (for engraved views of this district see the chapter on engraving); $40.00 – 65.00.

Plate 410: Engraved, Stock Exchange; St. Joseph, Missouri (rare); Watson; $40.00 – 80.00.

Plate 411: Engraved, New Casino; Santa Cruz, Calif.; Irving pattern; Wallace; $35.00 – 60.00.

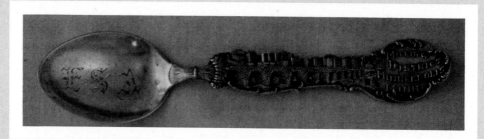

Plate 409

Plate 410

Plate 411

Plate 412: Silverplate souvenir of tour of Wallace Silver Manufactory; Wallace; $10.00 – 20.00. (Note: spoons are also available from other silver factories.)

Plate 413: Silverplate souvenir of tour of Wallace Silver Manufactory; Wallace; $10.00 – 20.00.

Plate 414: John Pierpont Morgan (1837 – 1913), (leading financier; ironically his policies led to the devaluation of silver as a precious metal); Dominick; $40.00 – 75.00.

Plate 412

Plate 413

Plate 414

Plate 415: Engraved, Krell, French Piano Factory, New Castle, Indiana; $40.00 – 70.00.

Plate 416: Engraved, furniture factory, Grand Rapids, Michigan; no manuf. mark; $30.00 – 50.00.

Plate 417: Engraved, Pearl Button Factory, Manchester, Ohio; Paye & Baker; $30.00 – 50.00.

Plate 415

Plate 416

Plate 417

Plate 418: Engraved, Abraham Straus Department Store; New York; Cabot pattern; completely gold washed; Wallace; $30.00 – 50.00.

Plate 419: Ophir Mine, Virginia City, Nev.; Old English pattern; Towle; $60.00 – 80.00.

Plate 420: Engraved, steam shovel; coal mining; $25.00 – 40.00.

Plate 421: Wanamaker, (major U.S. retailer and largest in N.Y. City); marked JW; $40.00 – 80.00.

Plate 418

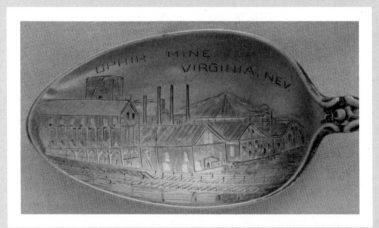

Plate 419

Plate 421

Plate 420

161

— Scientific Discoveries —

The basic physical principles of matter and energy were gradually disclosing their secrets. New scientific breakthroughs in most material areas led to new chemistry, new electrical development, new transportation, aerodynamics, and the list could easily be extended. Never before in history had so much scientific investigation yielded so many useful inventions in such a short period of time.

It is very difficult to depict many of these discoveries in a single image. Typically a building was selected which represented the scientific discovery. For example, the Lick Observatory in California was a favorite destination of tourists.

Spoons representing new scientific breakthroughs are fairly rare.

Plate 422: Tampa, Florida; (Jules Verne used Tampa as the launch site for a rocket to the moon in one of his novels more than 150 years before the federal government selected Cape Kennedy (Canaveral) as its primary launch site); Watson; $50.00 – 75.00.

Plate 423: Luther Burbank (1849 – 1926), (leading horticulturist); John Hood; $40.00 – 75.00.

Plate 424: Lick Observatory, San Jose, California; detail of bowl for Hyperion pattern in Plate 425.

Plate 423

Plate 422

Plate 424

Plate 425: Lick Observatory, San Jose, California, three engraved views. (James Lick donated $600,000 to build the world's largest telescope. The fifth moon of Jupiter was discovered in 1892.) Top: Engraved, Hyperion pattern, ca. 1905, grapefruit bowl; Whiting; $40.00 – 70.00; engraved; Whiting; $40.00 – 60.00; engraved; Pattern #4, ca. 1905; Wallace; $30.00 – 50.00.

Plate 426: Halley's Comet souvenir, ca. 1910; Manchester/Baker; $40.00 – 60.00.

Plate 425

Plate 426

Showing America's Future

Expositions became a primary method of demonstrating new technology and introducing arts and culture to the world. The Columbian Exposition of 1893 came shortly after the beginning of the souvenir spoon mania, and it is believed that more spoons were created for this single expo than for any other single event. One book has identified well over 300 different spoons or varieties commemorating this World's Fair.

The St. Louis Fair in 1903 was to celebrate the acquisition of the Louisiana Territory. In 1904, Portland celebrated the Lewis and Clark expedition. The Alaska Yukon Pacific Exposition in 1909 celebrated the mining industry and the growth of the western United States. The 1915 exposition in San Francisco and San Diego celebrated the completion of the Panama Canal, an event that changed the role of the entire western United States. We can find a number of very interesting spoons for all of these expositions.

A number of other minor expositions were held and souvenir spoons were created for each of these events. The pieces shown here are not meant to be exhaustive but merely to show the tremendous variety of spoons available to spooners and exposition collectors.

Spoons made for various expos range from very common to very rare.

— Columbian Exposition —
Chicago, 1893

Plate 427: Columbian World's Fair; Niagara Silver Co.; $40.00 – 75.00; no manuf. mark; $30.00 – 50.00; unidentified; $30.00 – 60.00.

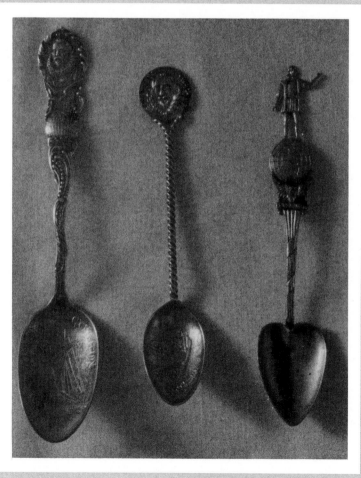

Plate 427

Plate 428: E. Pluribus Unum; Wallace; $100.00 – 150.00.

Plate 429: I Will Lady, detail; cloisonné and enamel; probably made in Austria for the Chicago Columbian World's Fair of 1893; $500.00+.

Plate 430: Columbus on a globe, mother-of-pearl bowl; no manuf. mark; $50.00 – 90.00.

Plate 431: Common silver plated demi; marked "AMN STERLING CO"; about $5.00. Note the deceptive marking. It is not sterling silver, that is the name of the company. Deceptions of this type are not common, but there are several companies that use them.

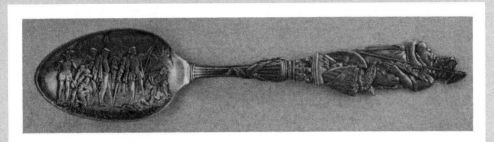

Plate 428

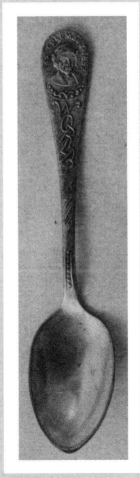

Plate 429   Plate 430   Plate 431

Plate 432: Chicago Columbian World's Fair. Top row: Alvin, $30.00 – 50.00; Watson, $30.00 – 50.00; Shepard, $30.00 – 50.00; Copyright Merlin, $20.00 – 40.00. Bottom row: no manuf. mark, $30.00 – 50.00; no manuf. mark, $30.00 – 50.00; Hyman Berg, $40.00 – 60.00.

Plate 432

Plate 433: Chicago Columbian World's Fair. Top row: Roger Bros, silver plate, $10.00 – 20.00; no manuf. mark, $30.00 – 50.00; no manuf. mark, $20.00 – 40.00; Alvin, $20.00 – 50.00. Bottom row: no manuf. mark, $30.00 – 50.00; Watson, $30.00 – 50.00; no manuf. mark, $25.00 – 50.00.

Plate 433

Plate 434: Rare mechanical globe; Woman's Building, Columbian World's Fair; $100.00 – 150.00.

Plate 435: Columbian World's Fair. Watson, $40.00 – 80.00; Alvin, $30.00 – 75.00; Dominick, $30.00 – 50.00; no mark, prob. silver-plated, $10.00 – 20.00; no manuf. mark, $25.00 – 40.00; Alvin, $20.00 – 40.00.

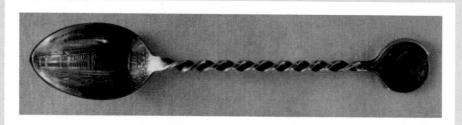

Plate 434

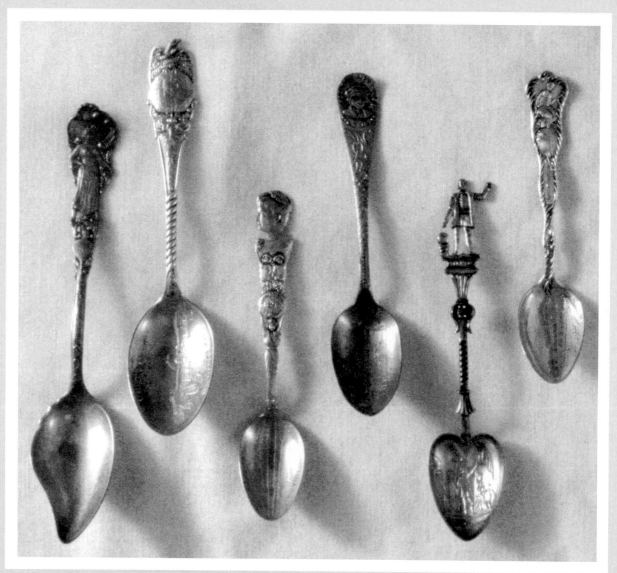

Plate 435

Plate 436: Columbian World's Fair souvenir tongs; no manuf. mark; $30.00 – 50.00.

Plate 437: Columbian World's Fair. Tilden Thorber, $40.00 – 80.00; Towle, $30.00 – 60.00; D. Low, $40.00 – 80.00; Watson, $40.00 – 80.00.

Plate 438: Mrs. Potter Palmer, aka Bertha Honore, (wife of a major Chicago financier and a leading planner for the 1893 Columbian World's Fair. She served on the board of lady managers and made the Woman's Building a notable success.); no manuf. mark; $50.00 – 85.00.

Plate 436

Plate 437

Plate 438

— Pan Pacific Exposition —
San Francisco, 1915

Plate 439: Palace of Horticulture; Watson; $40.00 – 60.00.

Plate 440: Tower of Jewels; Watson; $40.00 – 60.00.

Plate 439

Plate 440

Plate 441: Festival Hall; Watson; $40.00 – 60.00.

Plate 442: California Building; Meyer Bros.; $30.00 – 50.00.

Plate 441

Plate 442

Plate 443: Spoon and fork; Robbins; $100.00 set.

Plate 444: Robbins; $20.00 – 40.00.

Plate 445: Bear finial pipe; 1915; no manuf. mark; $20.00 – 35.00.

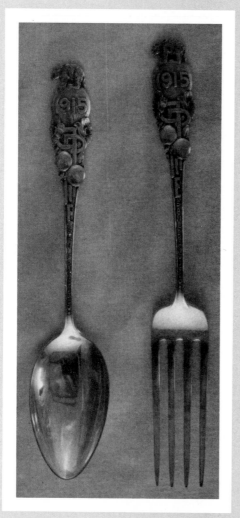

Plate 443

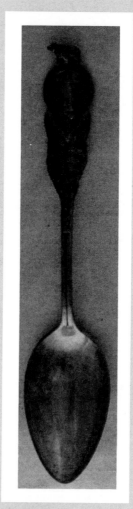

Plate 444

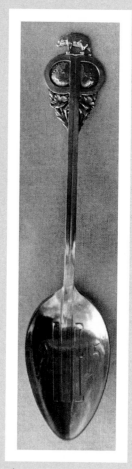

Plate 445

— Other Expos —

Plate 446: San Diego Expo, engraved, California Building 1915; J. Mayer Bros.; $40.00 – 60.00.

Plate 447: Louisiana Purchase Expo 1903; $1 U.S. gold coin in bowl; rare; copyright Bert Ball; $300.00+.

Plate 448: Seattle World's Fair 1967; copyright 1961; Century 21 Exposition, Inc.; sterling; $15.00 – 30.00.

Plate 449: Alaska Yukon Pacific Exposition (AYPE); Seattle, 1909. Totem pole with official emblem in bowl; note the round finial. This is actual gold from Alaska. It weighs ½ pennyweight; back marked "Indian Totem Pole, Alaska;" William Linker; $150.00 – 250.00. Official AYPE spoon; back of bowl marked "Official Souvenir Alaska Yukon Pacific Expo Approved" with the facsimile signatures of the president (of the expo) and the director general; J. Mayer Bros.; $30.00 – 50.00.

Plate 446

Plate 447

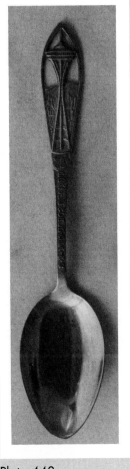

Plate 448

Plate 449

Plate 450: Engraved, Palace of Liberal Arts; Mechanics; $30.00 – 50.00.

Plate 451: Engraved, Cascade Gardens (the most pictured and notable part of the fair); $30.00 – 90.00.

Plate 452: Demi, enamel handle; Cotton States International Exposition, Atlanta, Ga.; Whiting; depending on handle, $20.00 – 45.00.

Plate 450

Plate 451

Plate 452

Plate 453: San Diego open-air pipe organ; 1915; plain bowl; $20.00 – 40.00.

Plate 454: Omaha Expo, painted enamel bowl; wavy handle; Shepard; $250.00 – 325.00.

Plate 455: Louisiana Purchase Expo spoons, ca. 1904. Napoleon and Jefferson, engraved Cascade Gardens bowl (see detail), Mermod Jacquard, $40.00 – 70.00; Palace of Liberal Arts (see detail), Mechanics, $30.00 – 50.00; Liberal Arts Building, Mechanics, $30.00 – 50.00; Machinist Building (see detail), Wallace, pattern #4, $30.00 – 50.00.

Plate 453

Plate 454

Plate 455

Plate 456: Demi, Pan Am1901; silver-plated; common; USSC; about $5.00.

Plate 457: Copper, Chicago World's Fair 1933; "official;" $5.00 – 10.00.

Plate 458: Engraved, Machinist Building; $30.00 – 50.00.

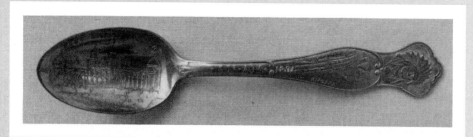

Plate 456

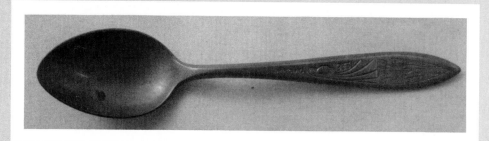

Plate 457

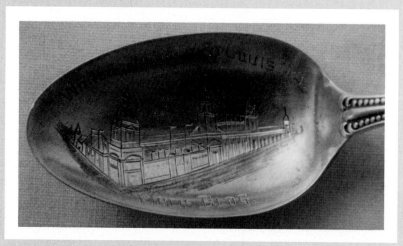

Plate 458

Plate 459: A number of cities built exposition halls to attract smaller shows. Engraved, Convention Hall; Kansas City; pat. Aug. 20, '96; $30.00 – 50.00 (fairly common). Engraved, Exposition Hall, Milwaukee; Whiting; $30.00 – 50.00.

Plate 460: Postcard, Convention Hall, Kansas City, Mo.

Plate 459

Plate 460

Inspiring Our Children

— Education —

The nature of work was rapidly changing. Since the dawn of civilization, most work was of a manual nature. A large percentage of the population was employed on the farm. Over the next century, this type of employment would continue to lose numbers.

New workers were required to have mind training and "book smarts." The growth of new knowledge in all areas made it necessary to pour increasing amounts of money into public education. Thousands of new schools were built to educate the future generations. Each small school was itself a triumph of persistence and necessity. Most of the small schools recorded on spoons were mementos of a student's successful completion of studies. Some were commemoratives of the school's establishment. The most common type of school found on spoons is the local high school. These are fairly common and inexpensive because there is not a large demand for them. But the quality of workmanship is usually very good. They were used as graduation souvenirs, fund raisers, gifts, and awards. College spoons are also frequently found because many of the people who attended were wealthier and could afford these higher-priced souvenirs. Elementary and specialized school spoons are much less common.

A collection of education-related spoons would be inexpensive and very interesting.

Plate 461: Generic spoons that were designed to be customized for each school and given to the graduate as a memento of the occasion. Male graduate is rarer than female version; enameled bowl; $40.00 – 80.00.

Plate 462: Generic female graduate spoons (large and small teaspoon); Mechanics; note customization date and initials on left and engraved picture on right; $30.00 – 70.00 each.

Plate 461

Plate 462

178

Plate 463: Engraved, Luther L. Wright School, Ironwood, Mich.; Cambridge pattern; Gorham; $10.00 – 40.00.

Plate 464: Engraved, Normal School, Stevens Point, Wis.; Shepard; $15.00 – 40.00.

Plate 465: Engraved, public school, Lyons, Neb.; Violet pattern, ca. 1905; Wallace; $15.00 – 40.00.

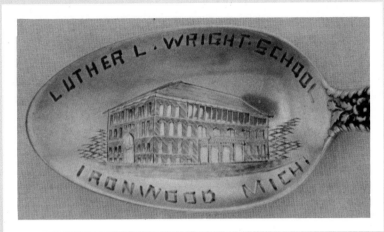

Plate 463

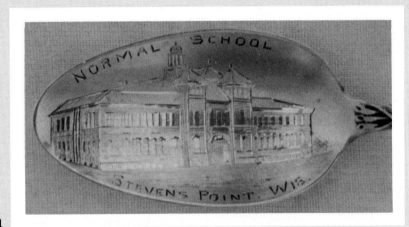

Plate 464

Plate 465

Plate 466: Engraved, Willett's School, Monmouth, Ill.; Melrose pattern; Gorham; $15.00 – 40.00.

Plate 467: Engraved, State Normal School, Dekalb, Ill.; Codding Bros; $15.00 – 40.00.

Plate 468: Engraved, school building, Mt. Ayr, Iowa; Lunt; $15.00 – 40.00.

Plate 466

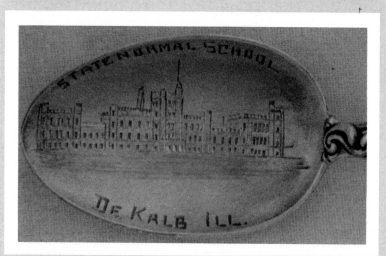

Plate 467

Plate 468

Plate 469: Engraved, high school, Pittsfield, Ill.; Cordova pattern; Towle; $15.00 – 40.00.

Plate 470: Engraved, high school, David City, Neb.; graduation handle; Wallace; $15.00 – 60.00.

Plate 471: Engraved, high school, Rapid City, South Dakota; Wild Rose pattern; Coddington; $15.00 – 40.00.

Plate 469

Plate 470

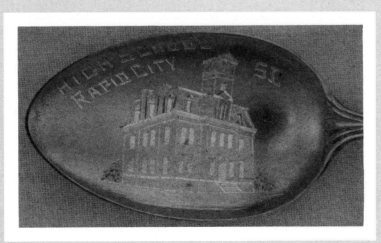

Plate 471

Plate 472: Engraved, high school, Eagle Grove, Iowa; Gorham; $15.00 – 40.00.

Plate 473: Engraved, high school, Burley, Idaho; Meyer Bros.; $15.00 – 40.00.

Plate 474: Engraved, high school, Holdrege, Neb.; Watson; $15.00 – 40.00.

Plate 472

Plate 473

Plate 474

Plate 475: Engraved, high school; Fort Atkinson; ca. 1897; Wendell; $15.00 – 40.00.

Plate 476: Engraved, high school; Greeley, Col.; Chantilly pattern; Gorham; $15.00 – 40.00.

Plate 477: Engraved, high school; Rockford, Ill.; graduation handle; Wallace; $40.00 – 60.00.

Plate 475

Plate 476

Plate 477

Plate 478: Samples of high school spoons; $15.00 – 60.00 each.

Plate 478

Plate 479: Engraved, new high school building; prob. a souvenir of the grand opening; Wallace; $30.00 – 50.00.

Plate 480: Engraved, University of Oklahoma, Norman; Louvre pattern; Wallace; $20.00 – 50.00.

Plate 481: Engraved, Stanford University Gate, Palo Alto; Calif.; J. Mayer Bros; $25.00 – 50.00.

Plate 479

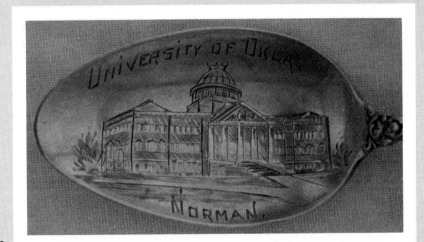

Plate 480

Plate 481

Plate 482: Engraved, Institute, Columbia, Tenn.; unidentified Art Nouveau handle; $20.00 – 50.00.

Plate 483: Engraved, Union University, Jackson, Tenn.; Watson; $20.00 – 50.00.

Plate 484: Engraved, Wesleyan Female College, Macon, Georgia; partial gold trimming; Elaine pattern; Lunt. The technique of partial gold gilding was new and is fairly rare. $40.00 – 60.00.

Plate 482

Plate 483

Plate 484

Plate 485: Engraved, University of Idaho, Moscow; Paye & Baker; $20.00 – 50.00.

Plate 486: Engraved, Allen Steinheim Alfred University, Alfred, New York; Paye & Baker; $25.00 – 50.00.

Plate 487: "Fair Harvard," stamped and engraved (building); back engraved initials and 1891; no manuf. mark; $35.00 – 70.00.

Plate 485

Plate 486

Plate 487

Plate 488: Engraved, coat of arms, Wentworth Hall, Jackson, New Hampshire; pattern 52; Shepard; $40.00 – 60.00.

Plate 489: Unusual potato fork, University of Illinois; $100.00 – 150.00.

Plate 488

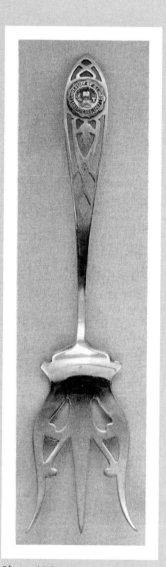

Plate 489

Plate 490: Various college spoons; $25.00 – 50.00 each.

Plate 490

Plate 491: Watson and Newell Co. catalog, ca. 1900 – 1910

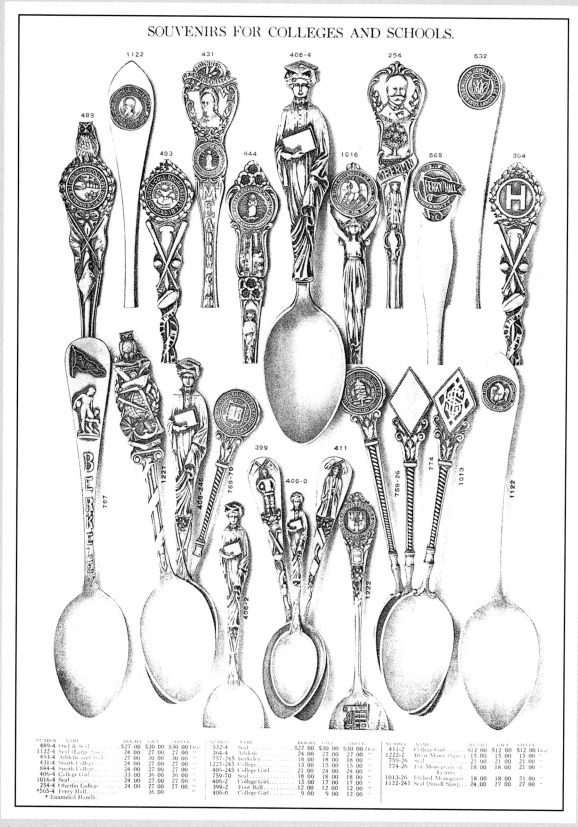

SOUVENIRS FOR COLLEGES AND SCHOOLS.

— Museums and Cultural Facilities —

Plate 492: Art Museum, Cincinnati; Mary Warren pattern; Baker Manchester; also Art Institute and Layton Art Gallery; Manchester/Baker; $25.00 – 50.00.

Plate 492

Plate 493: Engraved, Layton Art Gallery, Milwaukee; $25.00 – 50.00.

Plate 494: Engraved with bronze insert into silver; The Art Institute, Chicago; Watson; $50.00 – 100.00.

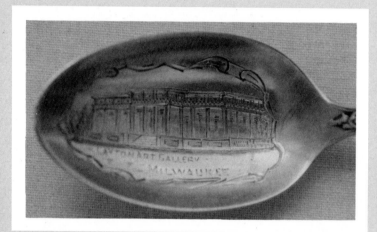

Plate 493

Plate 494

American Way of Life

—Sports —

Although every major manufacturer had a line of spoons directed at various sports, we do not find as many surviving sports spoon as we would expect.

Some of the spoons were designed to be given as awards and are usually highly prized by collectors. Others referring to a specific sport were often advertised as birthday presents.

Sports did not occupy the same position in society as they do today. Professional sports teams were only beginning to generate public attention and most sports activity spoons were directed toward individual participation.

Plate 495: Rodeo spoons. Top: embossed bowl; Dickinson 4 – 13 – '07 engraved on back; North Dakota state handle (was this a prize spoon?); Mechanics; $30.00 – 50.00. Left: Bronco rider finial; Hirsch & Oppenheimer; $30.00 – 50.00. Right: Bronco rider, plain bowl; no manuf. mark; $20.00 – 35.00.

Plate 495

Plate 496: Demi, bicycle advertising spoon; "Leads the Leaders;" (pleasure bicycling and bicycle races were very popular pastimes); Alvin & Waltham marks; $25.00 – 40.00.

Plate 497: Woman in bathing suit (risque); Paye & Baker; $75.00 – 125.00.

Plate 498: Woman diver; Watson; $75.00 – 100.00; woman diver; J. Mayer Bros.; $50.00 – 90.00.

Plate 499: Tennis racquet; (note hearts at top as a rebus for the tennis term "love"); Gorham; #582; $60.00 – 100.00.

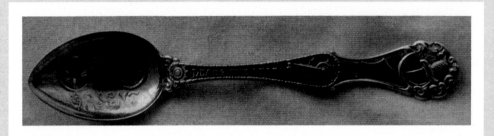

Plate 496

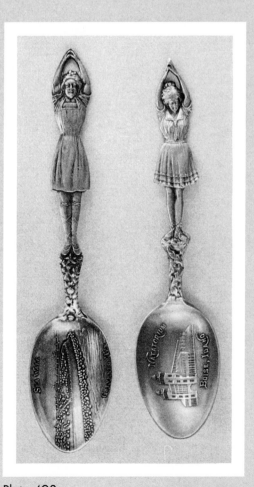

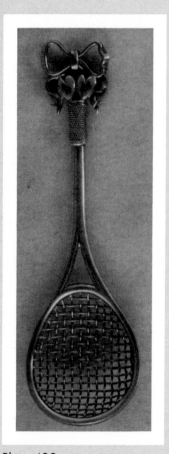

Plate 497

Plate 498

Plate 499

Plate 500: Horse raising (or racing); one of a kind and was probably a trophy for a race; (note the high quality workmanship, beautiful engraving, and bronze horse); handmade; no manuf. mark; $100.00 – 200.00.

Plate 501: Engraved, Broadwater Natatorium (indoor swimming pool); Helena, Montana; depending on handle, $30.00 – 60.00.

Plate 502: Engraved, Hanna Pool; Lampasas, Texas; SSMC; $30.00 – 50.00.

Plate 501

Plate 500

Plate 502

Plate 503: Engraved, spear fishing; also a rebus for Spearfish; South Dakota; Watson; $30.00 – 50.00.

Plate 504: Engraved, Outing Club, Davenport; Shepard; $30.00 – 75.00.

Plate 505: Engraved, Waveland Park Golf Club, Waveland, Indiana; (International Silver) Napoleon pattern; Wilcox mark; $40.00 – 75.00.

Plate 503

Plate 504

Plate 505

Plate 506: Engraved, ski jumping, Ishpeming, Mich; (note the detailed engraving); Watson; $75.00 – 100.00.

Plate 507: Demi, Indianapolis 500 (auto race); no manuf. mark; $15.00 – 25.00.

Plate 508: Tournament of Roses (Rose Parade); (Rose Bowl is the site of a major college football game every January 1); Pasadena, Calif.; prob. stainless steel; Robbins; $5.00 – 25.00.

Plate 506

Plate 507

Plate 508

— Fraternal Organizations —

Whenever things change quickly, there are always winners and losers. Men as a group began to feel that they were on the losing end of the dramatic changes that were affecting society. Males had been the dominant members of the family, and the respected breadwinners. But as women began to be more assertive and earn outside income, the balance of power was shifting. Women were playing increasingly important roles in society and the educationally emancipated daughters were no longer the "dutiful little girls."

Many men felt it necessary to preserve aspects of their importance. They began to retreat into private male-only clubs. During the 1890s, hundreds of these clubs and fraternities were created in every town to help men restore their "lost glory." Typically, fraternal organizations would build nice buildings with bars or golf or tennis clubs and rooms which were decorated in "male approved styles" rather than the female chintz in which most Victorian homes were decorated.

These fraternal gathering places ranged from one room to large scale buildings, but all of them were of importance to the local culture, often playing an important role in business and government operations. The silver spoons shown illustrate the importance of the male-only clubs.

Women formed their own civic organizations, involving themselves in charity work, preserving historical buildings, creating museums, and creating a social atmosphere that balanced the demands made by men in their economic-oriented organizations. Many spoons honor the various women's clubs, historical buildings they preserved, and other activities.

A wide variety of spoons relating to fraternal organizations are available.

Plate 509: Engraved, Masonic Temple, Toledo, Ohio; Cloeta pattern, ca. 1905; International; (note: the camera was tilted slightly, creating the strange roofline in the picture). $25.00 – 40.00.

Plate 509

Plate 510: Engraved, Masonic Temple, Chicago; untraced manuf.; $30.00 – 50.00. (This building is represented on many spoons. Most bowls are embossed. There is a lot of detail engraved in this bowl.)

Plate 511: DAR, temple in bowl; Krider; $50.00 – 75.00.

Plate 512: Convention souvenir, Knights of Pythias; Pairpoint; $30.00 – 50.00.

Plate 513: Mrs. Babs, PEO (secret code); Alvin; $30.00 – 60.00.

Plate 510

Plate 511

Plate 512

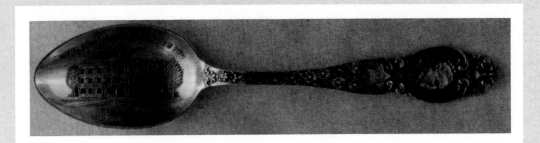

Plate 513

Plate 514: Cornelia Fairbanks, DAR; J.E. Caldwell; $40.00 – 75.00.

Plate 515: Enameled fork and spoon finials, Order of Eastern Star; Wm. B. Kerr; $75.00 – 125.00 set.

Plate 516: Knights of Pythias; Watson; $30.00 – 75.00.

Plate 517: BPOE, Protective Brotherhood of Elk; Gorham; $25.00 – 50.00.

Plate 514

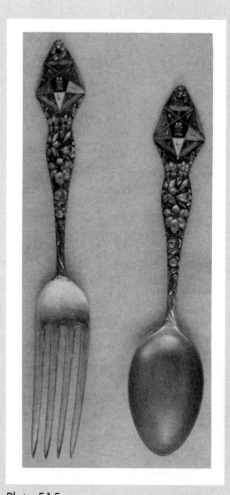

Plate 515

Plate 516

Plate 517

— Religion —

Religion has always played an important part in American life. The Pilgrims settled in this country to avoid religious persecution at home.

Silver apostle spoons have been made since the sixteenth century. One of the apostles would be pictured on the the spoon finial. These were usually given to babies upon their baptism. The phrase "to be born with a silver spoon" stems from this tradition. Apostle spoons have long been collectible and Gorham issued a series during the spoon movement.

During the 1800s numerous new religions and offshoots of established religions were created. Some of these tried to create utopian communities and others developed their own rituals. Most of these new religions eventually collapsed, but some have emerged to become established mainstream religions.

Many of the colonial churches are represented on spoons. These old buildings have an important historical facet to them as well as a religious one. Many churches were built with stunning architectural elements. The sheer beauty and majesty of the building are often depicted on spoons.

In addition, many smaller churches would have pictures of their new building engraved on spoons. These were sold to the local parishoners as commemoratives of their new building. Sometimes church spoons were also used as fund raisers.

For the religious-oriented spoon collector, this collecting niche would produce a significant collection.

Plate 518: Engraved, chicken laying egg, Easter, demi; $15.00 – 25.00.

Plate 519: Ramona's Marriage Place, San Diego, Calif. (Note: Many different versions of Ramona's Marriage Place are available.) $20.00 – 30.00.

Plate 518

Plate 519

Plate 520: Trumpet, Bethlehem; Gorham; $50.00 – 75.00.

Plate 521: "The Ascension;" Wallace; $100.00 – 150.00.

Plate 522: "Luther knocking at the door;" unidentified maker but prob. American; German wording; $40.00 – 75.00.

Plate 523: Apostles; Gorham; 1890s; $200.00+ each.

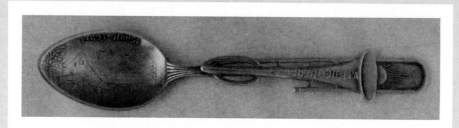

Plate 520

Plate 521

Plate 522

Plate 523

Plate 524: Apostles; Gorham; reissue 1974; $50.00 – 75.00 each.

Plate 525: Apostles, Gorham, reverse. Left: mark from 1890s on both sides of "rattail." Right: mark from 1974 reissue; only on right of "rattail."

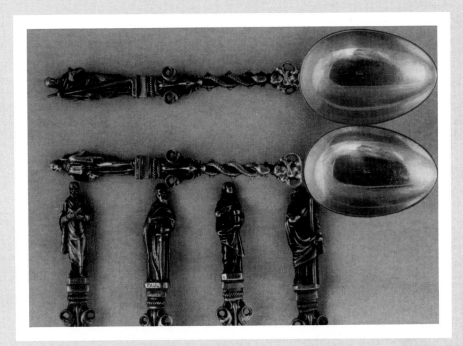

Plate 524

Plate 525

Plate 526: Devil, with unusual bronzing; bowl, French Lick Hotel; $100.00 – 150.00; Virgin and Child; Ramona's Marriage Place, San Diego, Calif.; $50.00 – 75.00.

Plate 527: Reverse of above.

Plate 527

Plate 526

Plate 528: Santa Claus; Johnston & Co.; $100.00 – 150.00; Mechanics, $75.00 – 100.00; Meyer Brothers, reissue; $30.00 – 50.00; engraved date "1892;" $45.00 – 65.00.

Plate 529: St. Louis Cathedral, New Orleans; Paye & Baker; $30.00 – 75.00.

Plate 529

Plate 528

Plate 530: St. John; Shiebler; $500.00+.

Plate 531: Reverse of above.

Plate 532: Engraved, Grace Episcopal Church, Cortland, New York; Newbury pattern, ca. 1900; gold washed; Towle; $15.00 – 30.00.

Plate 530

Plate 531

Plate 532

Plate 533: Christmas chimney scene; Mechanics; $35.00 – 50.00; Santa Claus; Mechanics; $30.00 – 40.00.

Plate 534: Devil, bowl/Garfield Monument, Cleveland; Alsirat Grotto; Watson; $95.00 – 150.00.

Plate 533

Plate 534

Plate 535: Holly; Wallace; $25.00 – 40.00; demi; Chimney; Gorham; $15.00 – 25.00; demi; Virgin; $15.00 – 25.00.

Plate 536: DeWitt Talmadge (1832 – 1902), (Dutch Reformed Church, known as a "brilliant sensationalist preacher"); Gorham; $40.00 – 75.00.

Plate 535

Plate 536

Plate 537: Engraved, Reid Memorial Church, Richmond, Indiana; Fessenden; $20.00 – 40.00.

Plate 538: Postcard, Reid Memorial Church, Richmond, Ind.

Plate 537

Plate 538

Plate 539: Engraved, Presbyterian Church, Hastings, Nebraska; Colfax pattern; Gorham; $15.00 – 30.00.

Plate 540: Engraved, M.E. Church, Sikeston, Missouri; flower pattern; Paye & Baker; $15.00 – 30.00.

Plate 541: Engraved, M.E. Church, Portland, Indiana; Watson; $15.00 – 30.00.

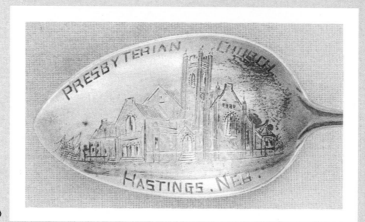

Plate 539

Plate 540

Plate 541

Plate 542: Rare and unusual handmade, one of a kind ceremonial spoon; marked "sterling silver;" gold plated bowl $300.00+.

Plate 543: Varder Lincoln, president 1st Presbyterian Church; Shiebler; $35.00 – 70.00.

Plate 544: Engraved, Church of the Good Shepherd, Momence, Illinois; Rose pattern, ca. 1898; Wallace; $15.00 – 30.00.

Plate 542

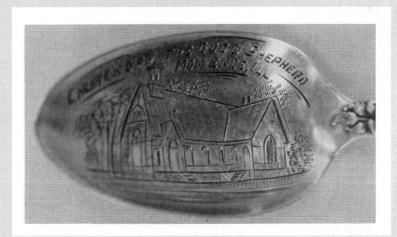

Plate 544

Plate 543

Plate 545: Jewish spoon showing various symbols; silver-plated; Michael C. Fina Co., New York. (This is the only American Jewish religion spoon I have seen.) $10.00 – 25.00.

Plate 546: Engraved, pipe organ, First Presbyterian Church; Two Harbors, Minnesota; Simon Brothers, ca. 1900; rare; $75.00 – 125.00.

Plate 547: Withrow, 3rd Presbyterian Church, died 1892; no manuf. mark; $30.00 – 50.00.

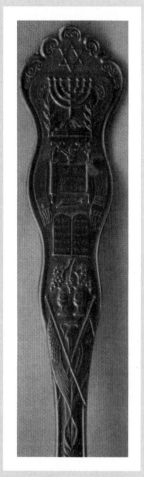

Plate 545

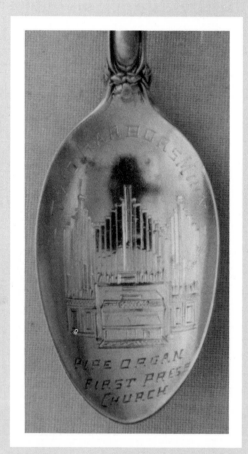

Plate 546

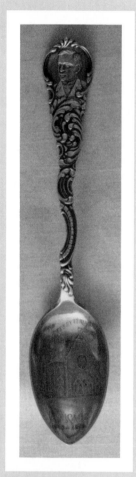

Plate 547

— Societal Eccentricities —

Today we view the late Victorians through the perspective of our own culture, but we should try to understand their culture before we cast aspersions on it. The late Victorians had some ideas and theories that we today might find offensive or exceedingly strange. In addition to their negative depiction of black people, some of the native Indian tribes also take offense at some of the Indian spoons.

Today our concepts of "politically correct" thinking and speech are contrary to some of the ideas and stereotypes turn-of-the-century society accepted as gospel. Spoons depicting black people are very stereotyped. At this time, these pieces are very highly prized and collectible and they command very high prices. I do not understand the reason for this as these pieces are neither particularly rare nor better examples of Victorian life, but I cannot second guess the market.

Other times we find strange customs on spoons. The enlarged picture showing a woman nursing a baby by holding it to a goat's udder is very strange and foreign to our way of thinking.

Labors of Cupid, Love Disarmed, and depictions of an imaginary "old world" were all part and parcel of the way of life. Even today as we admire the beauty and grace of life on a great Southern plantation, we forget this life was made possible by the sweat of slaves. We cannot change the past, only understand and learn from it.

Plate 548: Engraved detail, "Children being nursed with goat's milk;" (look closely and you can see the mother holding the child up to the goat's udder); enameled finial; Shepard; $100.00 – 125.00.

Plate 549: New Orleans, enamel bowl, painted, with three black men; Watson; $225.00 – 300.00.

Plate 548

Plate 549

Plate 550: Black boy eating watermelon in bowl and squirrel at top; Watson; $95.00 – 125.00; full spoon; Shiebler; $85.00 – 125.00; black boy eating watermelon, cattail finial; Paye & Baker; $100.00 – 125.00.

Plate 551: Detail of center spoon Plate 550. Large black male, finial "Sunny South;" Shiebler; $85.00 – 125.00.

Plate 552: Black cotton picker in bowl, Crescent City, New Orleans handle; Paye & Baker, $125.00 – 175.00.

Plate 550

Plate 551

Plate 552

Plate 553: Enamel bowl, painted, watermelon with a black person finial; Gorham; $125.00 – 200.00.

Plate 554: Enameled black woman; Mechanics; $100.00 – 125.00; demi; full figure, black boy eating watermelon; demi; $75.00 – 125.00; Florida, black male and alligator; no manuf. mark; $80.00 – 100.00.

Plate 555: Rebus spoon, "spooning;" wavy handled state; Shepard; $75.00 – 100.00.

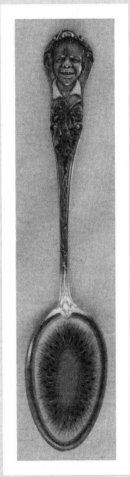

Plate 553

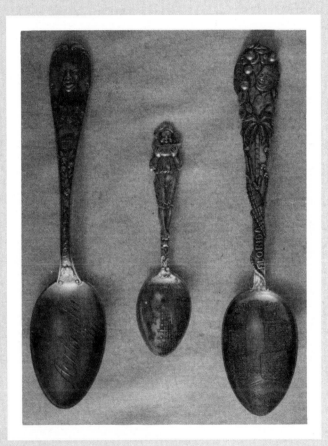

Plate 554

Plate 555

Plate 556: Demi, transfer print, Lincoln freeing the slaves; transfer print finial of White House; made in Germany for Albert H. Oechsle, Jefferson, Missouri; $30.00 – 75.00.

Plate 557: Florida, black boy eating watermelon, alligator and picture of Mechanic Street in the bowl; Mechanics; $150.00 – 190.00; figure of black boy eating watermelon and picture of New Orleans in the bowl; no manuf. mark; $150.00 – 190.00; Hot Springs, Arkansas, black male eating watermelon; SSMC; $100.00 – 125.00.

Plate 556

Plate 557

Plate 558: Cocaine Spoons (or for the squeamish, "ear spoons"); a third tool was attached at one time. No marks; $30.00 – 75.00; sensuous Art Nouveau nude; no marks; $15.00 – 30.00; U.S. Standing Liberty half dollar, dated 1946; hand cut-outs of design; no marks; $25.00 – 75.00.

Plate 559: Unusual coat of arms engraved with a German inscription. It has been translated as "The Christian's heart is inclined to the rose even when it stands under a cross;" Dominick & Haff; $50.00 – 75.00.

Plate 559

Plate 558

Note: Cocaine production and consumption were major problems during the 1890s and the drug was often used as an ingredient in many medicines, beverages, and other products. Many of our current drug laws date from this period. The purchase of drug paraphernalia may be illegal under some circumstances, so exercise caution.

Plate 560: Nürnberg series; Gorham; $25.00 – 50.00 each.

Plate 560

Plate 561: Nürnberg series; Gorham; $25.00 – 50.00 each.

Plate 562: Nursing mother on very long handled spoon with rose in bowl; given by Heinz Company to employees who had babies; Cartier; $200.00 – 400.00.

Plate 561

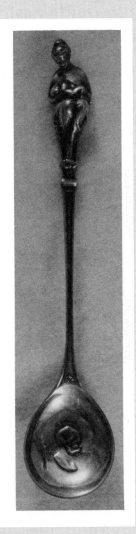

Plate 562

Plate 563: Labors of Cupid; Dominick & Haff; $40.00 – 100.00 each.

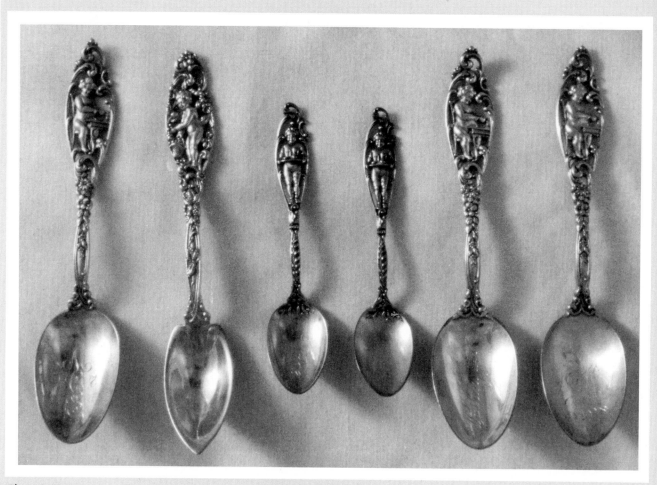

Plate 563

Plate 564: Love Disarmed, salad set; Reed & Barton; $400.00 – 600.00 set.

Plate 565: Labors of Cupid; Dominick & Haff; $75.00 – 150.00 each

Plate 564

Plate 565

Note: Some spoons and serving pieces in this style were reproduced in 1996 – 1997 using the same molds and are indistinguishable from the originals. The company has promised to mark new reproductions (if any) in the future. Let the buyer beware. These pieces are from an old collection.

Plate 566: "Old World" coffee spoons; Gorham; $35.00 – 60.00 each.

Plate 566

Plate 567: "Old World" coffee spoons; Gorham; $35.00 – 60.00 each.

Plate 567

Plate 568: Engraved, commemorative of a disaster, "Iroquois Theatre Burned Dec. 30 1903 595 Lives Lost Chicago;" Mechanics; $20.00 – 75.00.

Plate 569: King and Queen of Hearts; Watson; $125.00 – 150.00 each.

Plate 568

Plate 569

Plate 570: Watson and Newell Co. catalog, ca. 1900 – 1910.

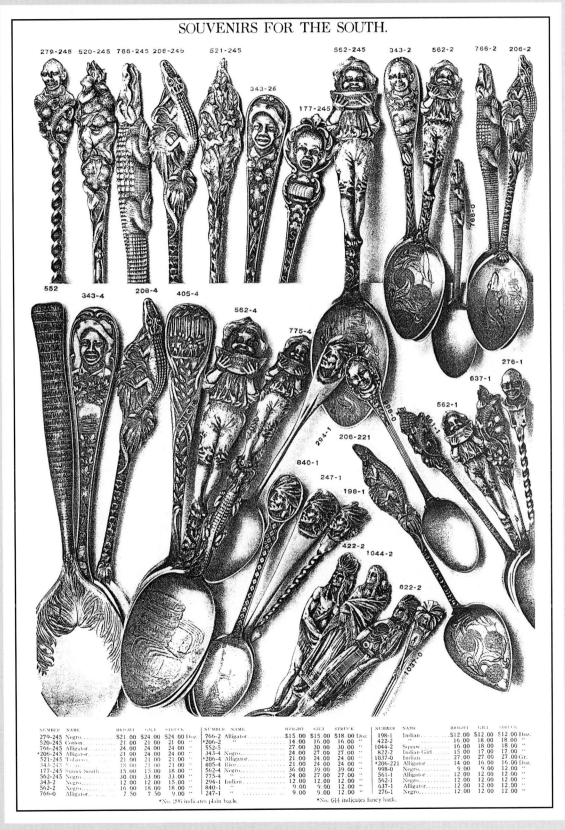

Plate 570

225

Plate 571: Watson and Newell Co. catalog, ca. 1900 – 1910.

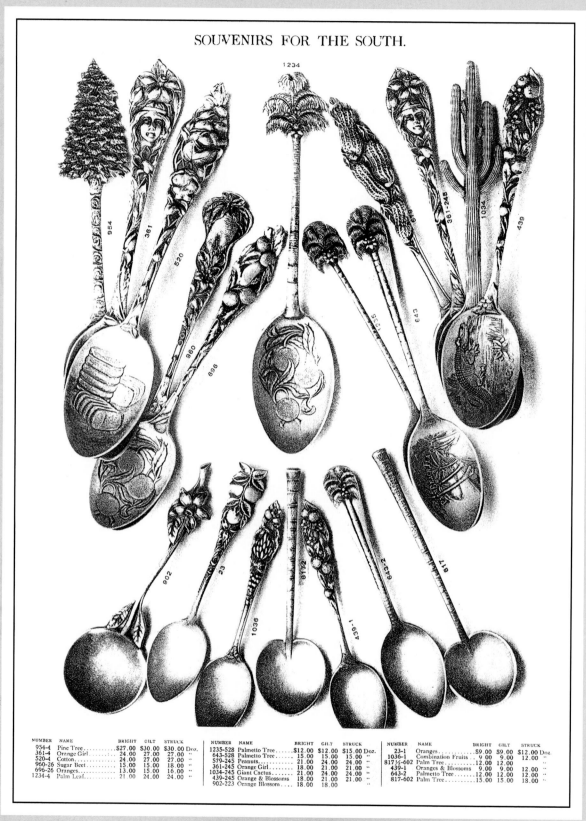

SOUVENIRS FOR THE SOUTH.

NUMBER	NAME	BRIGHT	GILT	STRUCK
954-4	Pine Tree	$27.00	$30.00	$30.00 Doz.
361-4	Orange Girl	24.00	27.00	27.00 "
520-4	Cotton	24.00	27.00	27.00 "
960-26	Sugar Beet	15.00	15.00	18.00 "
696-26	Oranges	13.00	15.00	16.00 "
1234-4	Palm Leaf	21.00	24.00	24.00 "

NUMBER	NAME	BRIGHT	GILT	STRUCK
1235-528	Palmetto Tree	$12.00	$12.00	$15.00 Doz.
643-528	Palmetto Tree	15.00	15.00	15.00 "
579-245	Peanuts	21.00	24.00	24.00 "
361-245	Orange Girl	18.00	21.00	21.00 "
1034-245	Giant Cactus	21.00	24.00	24.00 "
439-245	Orange & Blossoms	18.00	21.00	21.00 "
902-223	Orange Blossom	18.00	18.00	

NUMBER	NAME	BRIGHT	GILT	STRUCK
23-1	Oranges	$9.00	$9.00	$12.00 Doz.
1036-1	Combination Fruits	9.00	9.00	12.00 "
817½-602	Palm Tree	12.00	12.00	
439-1	Oranges & Blossoms	9.00	9.00	12.00 "
643-2	Palmetto Tree	12.00	12.00	12.00 "
817-602	Palm Tree	15.00	15.00	18.00 "

Plate 571

– Animals and Plants –

Victorians were extremely interested in the natural world. Many spoons depict animals, plants and flowers.

Animal spoons are very interesting for a variety of reasons. Sometimes the animal is used as a symbol to represent something else. For example we frequently find bears representing the State of California (the Bear Republic). Fish often represented a significant fishing industry. Storks represent newborns.

Plants and gardening activities were very popular. Every major estate had extensive gardens and most smaller homes also raised vegetables or flowers. We finds thousands of different spoons with corn, grains, trees, cactus, etc. It would be very easy for a person to specialize in any of these areas.

There was also a significant societal preoccupation with flowers. Many new varieties of flowers were bred during this time and the prevailing Art Nouveau trends placed great emphasis on flowers. Every manufacturer made a large number of flower-handled spoons. In addition, many of the flatware patterns featured flowers. I suspect there are more types of flower spoons available than any other single category.

For those interested in botany, souvenir spoon collecting would be an ideal method of creating a significant collection of silver flowers.

Plate 572: Oregon salmon; J. Mayer Brothers; $30.00 – 60.00; tuna; Paye & Baker; $25.00 – 50.00; Boston, baked beans and other symbols; Homer; $25.00 – 50.00.

Plate 573: Gray's Harbor Salmon; no manuf. mark; $25.00 – 50.00.

Plate 572

Plate 573

Plate 574: Whale in bowl, whaling ship finial; Gorham; $75.00 – 100.00.

Plate 575: Cape Cod; A. W. Flue; $30.00 – 50.00; New London; CBH; $30.00 – 50.00.

Plate 576: Columbia River salmon, demi, engraved webfoot; no manuf. mark; $20.00 – 40.00; Alaska salmon, plain bowl; no manuf. mark; $20.00 – 40.00; Chinook salmon; no manuf. mark; $15.00 – 25.00.

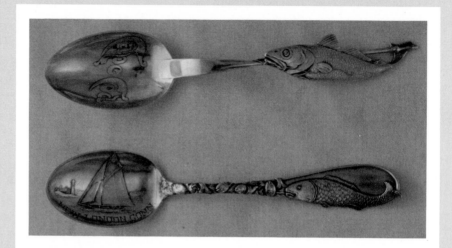

Plate 575

Plate 574

Plate 576

Plate 577: Mother-of-pearl fish bowls; silver-plated handles; no marks; $10.00 – 20.00 each.

Plate 578: Fish bowl; Gorham; $30.00 – 50.00; sea horse; Union; no quality mark; $10.00 – 30.00.

Plate 579: Turtle bowl, unusual; untraced manuf.; $30.00 – 75.00.

Plate 577

Plate 578

Plate 579

Plate 580: New Bedford whaling; G.E. Woodworth; $40.00 – 75.00.

Plate 581: Kodiak Bear family, plain bowl, no manuf. mark; $125.00 – 175.00; buffalo, Mechanics; $30.00 – 60.00.

Plate 582: Ostriches (ostrich farming was a new activity). Mt. Lowe Railroad; no manuf. mark; $25.00 – 50.00; apple picker; J.Mayer Brothers; $75.00 – 125.00; Fessenden; $30.00 – 50.00; Shepard; $30.00 – 50.00.

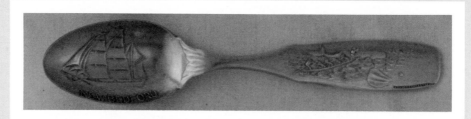

Plate 580

Plate 581

Plate 582

Plate 583: Storks (often used as birth spoons); Robbins, $25 – 40; Reed & Barton; $30.00 – 50.00; no manuf. mark; $30.00 – 50.00.

Plate 584: Engraved, San Diego, Calif.; Plymouth pattern, ca. 1900; Gorham; $30.00 – 50.00.

Plate 583

Plate 584

Plate 585: Three variations of stork spoons; Mauser; $20.00 – 70.00.

Plate 586: Stork; Watson; $30.00 – 60.00; Lunt; $30.00 – 60.00.

Plate 586

Plate 585

Plate 587: "Emblem of Happiness," from a play ca. 1907; Wallace; $10.00 – 20.00.

Plate 588: Ostrich grouping; Fessenden; $30.00 – 50.00.

Plate 589: Eagle, "Old Abe;" Gorham; rare; $300.00+.

Plate 587

Plate 589

Plate 588

Plate 590: "Hear no evil, see no evil, speak no evil;" plain bowl; Paye & Baker; $40.00 – 80.00.

Plate 591: Mule; "You will have to show me, I'm from Missouri;" plain bowl, Watson; $20.00 – 40.00.

Plate 592: Engraved, seal rocks, San Francisco, Calif.; Watson; $30.00 – 50.00.

Plate 593: "Who Killed Cock Robin," (from a book); baby spoon; $15.00 – 30.00.

Plate 591

Plate 590

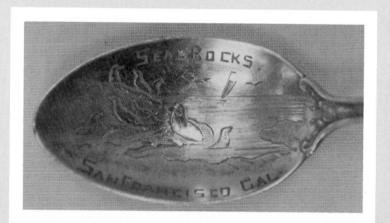

Plate 592

Plate 593

Plate 594: California bear, plain bowl; Shiebler; $75.00 – 125.00.

Plate 595: Webfoot full figural handle, Mechanics, $85.00 – 125.00; engraved cow, "Pride of the State," cow finial; no manuf. mark; $30.00 – 70.00.

Plate 596: San Gabriel Mission; Paye & Baker; $30.00 – 50.00.

Plate 596

Plate 595

Plate 594

Plate 597: Pine tree; Watson, $75.00 – 150.00; redwood; Meyer Brothers; $75.00 – 150.00; sequoia; no manuf. mark; $75.00 – 150.00.

Plate 598: Fir; Watson; $75.00 – 150.00; palm; no manuf. mark; $20.00 – 50.00; banana; no manuf. mark; possibly from Philippines, $20.00 – 40.00.

Plate 597

Plate 598

Plate 599: Palm; Dominick; $30.00 – 50.00; palm; Watson; $30.00 – 50.00; palm; LDA; $30.00 – 50.00.

Plate 600: Palm, Palm Beach, Florida; G&C Co.; reverse; $45.00 – 70.00.

Plate 599

Plate 600

Plate 601: Engraved, corn on railroad car, unusual; Lunt; $30.00 – 75.00.

Plate 602: Fruits; 13 in set; Watson; 500.00+ set, $20.00 – 40.00 each.

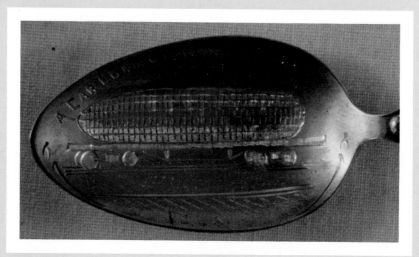

Plate 601

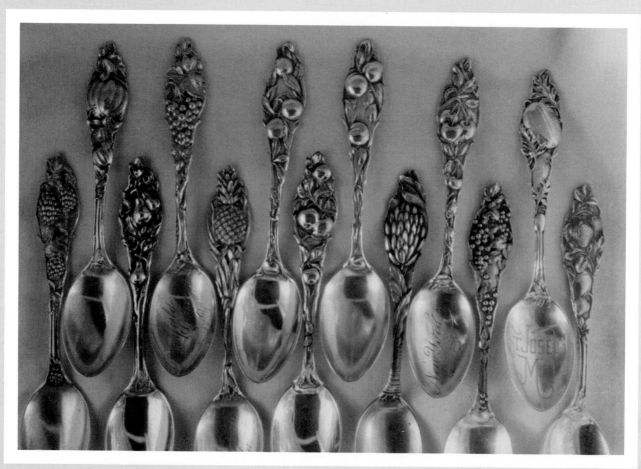

Plate 602

Plate 603: Flowers, Simpson Hall; January through June (marked on back); $20.00 – 40.00 each.

Plate 604: Flowers, Simpson Hall; July through December (July marked "7," others have month marked on the back); $20.00 – 40.00 each.

Plate 603

Plate 604

Plate 605: Enameled corn, Muscatine; $40.00 – 75.00; Watson; $25.00 – 40.00; Jose Straker Jr., gold washed and enameled; Watson; $40.00 – 75.00.

Plate 606: Mitchell Corn Palace, Mitchell, South Dakota; Paye & Baker; $30.00 – 60.00 each.

Plate 605

Plate 606

Plate 607: Grain flower finial, Minehaha Falls in bowl; Fessenden; $30.00 – 60.00.

Plate 608: Enameled flowers; no manuf. mark; prob. Shepard; $25.00 – 50.00 each.

Plate 609: Grape Pattern bon bon spoon; Mechanics; $40.00 – 70.00.

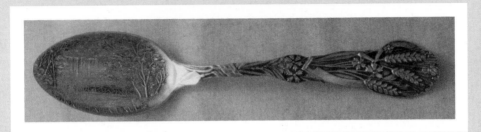

Plate 607

Plate 608

Plate 609

Plate 610: Engraved Bitter Root, Hamilton, Montana; Lunt; $30.00 – 50.00.

Plate 611: Floral Series; Wallace; #128 – 133; marked on back; $20.00 – 40.00 each.

Plate 610

Plate 611

Plate 612: Corn finial; Manchester/Baker; $25.00 – 50.00; corn finial on customized bowl; no manuf. mark, $40.00 – 60.00; corn finial on twisted handle; no manuf. mark, $30.00 – 50.00.

Plate 613: Floral series; Wallace; #134 – 139; marked on back; $20.00 – 40.00.

Plate 612

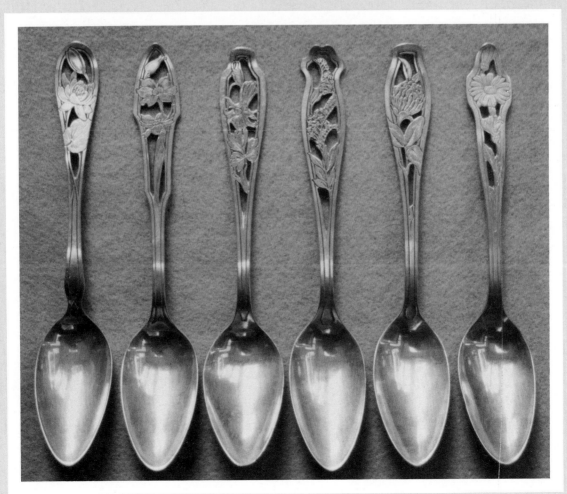

Plate 613

Plate 614: Peanuts; Mechanics; $40.00 – 75.00.

Plate 615: Prickly pear, Mexican coin bowl; Shreve; $60.00 – 100.00; cactus; Tammen; $30.00 – 60.00; cactus; M.F. Vantilburg; $30.00 – 60.00.

Plate 616: Cactus; Watson; $40.00 – 80.00; cactus; SSMC; $30.00 – 60.00

Plate 615

Plate 614

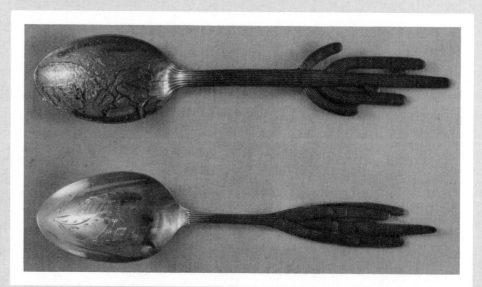

Plate 616

Plate 617: Sunflower; Kemper Armitage; Tiffany; $60.00 – 90.00.

Plate 618: Cactus, Arizona, enclosed; no manuf. mark; $15.00 – 30.00; same spoon with cactus in cut-out, Tammen; $20.00 – 40.00; Cook & Bell; Gorham; Prescott, Arizona, Casa Grande ruins in bowl; $40.00 – 80.00

Plate 619: Engraved, oranges, Los Angeles; Rose pattern, ca. 1898; Wallace; $30.00 – 60.00.

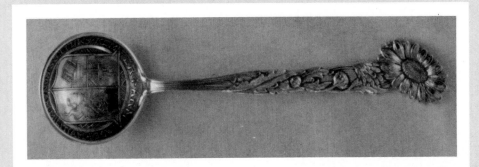

Plate 617

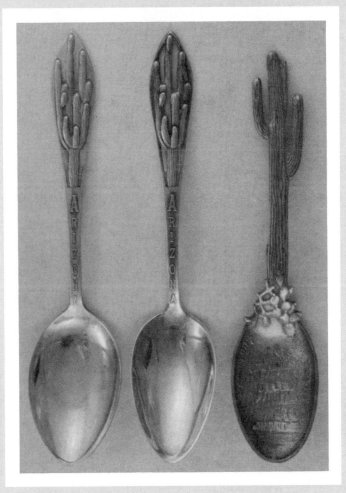

Plate 618

Plate 619

Plate 620: Engraved carrot (possibly sugar beet), Garden City, Kansas; no manuf. mark; $30.00 – 50.00.

Plate 621: Corn design; Paye & Baker; $20.00 – 40.00; corn stalk; Mechanics; $25.00 – 40.00; corn finial; Paye & Baker; $25.00 – 40.00.

Plate 620

Plate 621

Plate 622: Watson and Newell Co. catalog, ca. 1900 – 1910.

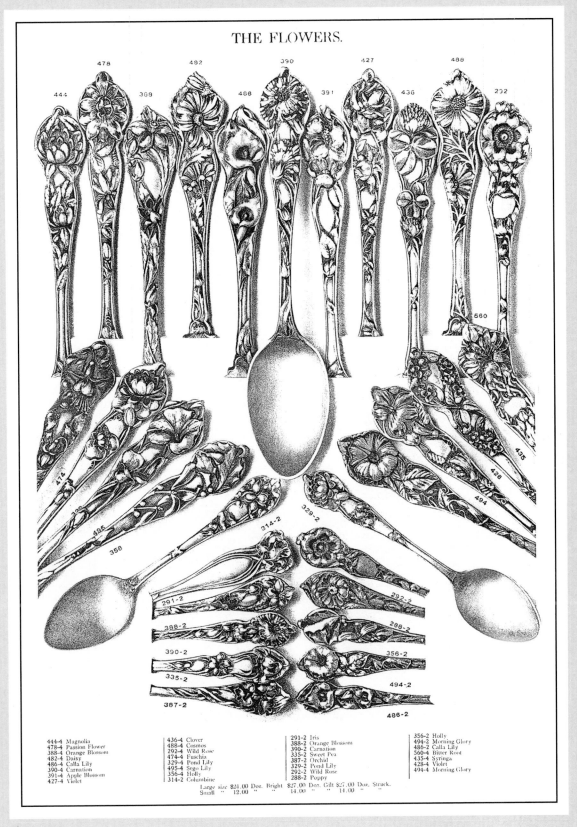

THE FLOWERS.

444-4 Magnolia	436-4 Clover	291-2 Iris	356-2 Holly
478-4 Passion Flower	488-4 Cosmos	388-2 Orange Blossom	494-2 Morning Glory
388-4 Orange Blossom	292-4 Wild Rose	390-2 Carnation	486-2 Calla Lily
482-4 Daisy	474-4 Fuschia	335-2 Sweet Pea	560-4 Bitter Root
486-4 Calla Lily	329-4 Pond Lily	387-2 Orchid	435-4 Syringa
390-4 Carnation	495-4 Sego Lily	329-2 Pond Lily	428-4 Violet
391-4 Apple Blossom	356-4 Holly	292-2 Wild Rose	494-4 Morning Glory
427-4 Violet	314-2 Columbine	288-2 Poppy	

Large size $24.00 Doz. Bright $27.00 Doz. Gilt $27.00 Doz. Struck.
Small   "   12.00   "   "   14.00   "   "   14.00   "   "

Plate 622

247

Plate 623: Watson and Newell Co. catalog, ca. 1900 – 1910.

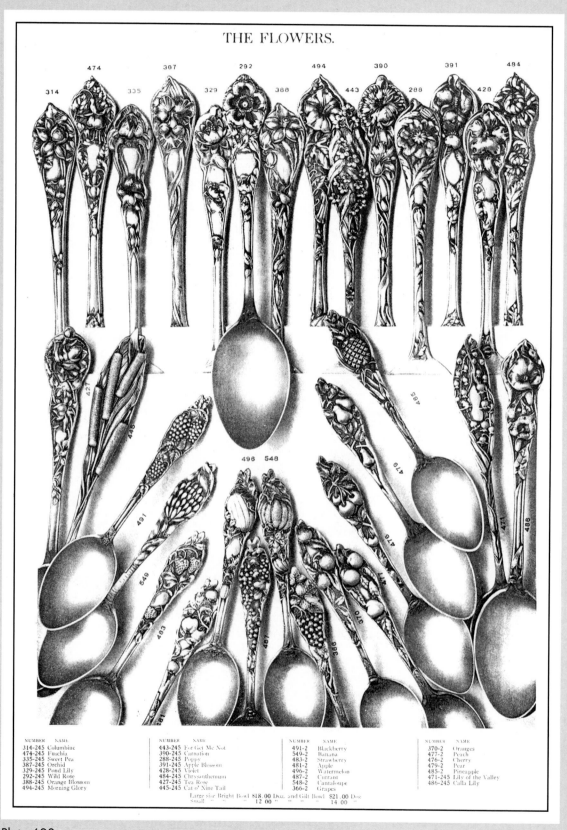

Plate 623

248

Plate 624: Watson and Newell Co. catalog, ca. 1900 – 1910.

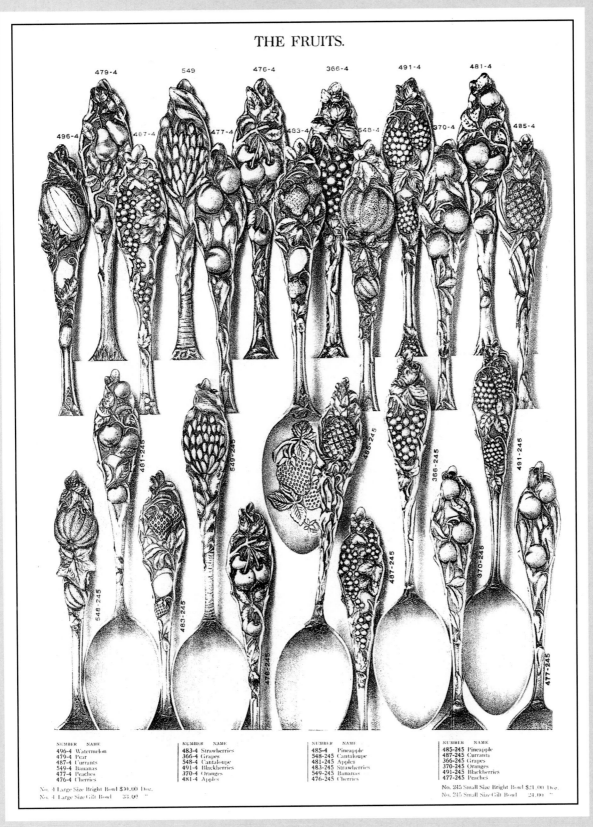

THE FRUITS.

NUMBER	NAME	NUMBER	NAME	NUMBER	NAME	NUMBER	NAME
496-4	Watermelon	483-4	Strawberries	485-4	Pineapple	485-245	Pineapple
479-4	Pear	366-245	Grapes	548-245	Cantaloupe	487-245	Currants
487-4	Currants	548-4	Cantaloupe	481-245	Apples	366-245	Grapes
549-4	Bananas	491-4	Blackberries	483-245	Strawberries	370-245	Oranges
477-4	Peaches	370-4	Oranges	549-245	Bananas	491-245	Blackberries
476-4	Cherries	481-4	Apples	476-245	Cherries	477-245	Peaches

No. 4 Large Size Bright Bowl $30.00 Doz.
No. 4 Large Size Gilt Bowl   33.00 "

No. 245 Small Size Bright Bowl $21.00 Doz.
No. 245 Small Size Gilt Bowl   24.00 "

Plate 624

— Hotels —

For a weary traveler, a hotel room with a warm bath and snug bed is wonderful. During the last part of the nineteenth century, hotels became ever larger and grander and some eventually became the destination as well as a room and bath. Throughout the country, a few of these old hotels still stand, but most of them have been destroyed or rebuilt to keep them current with the times. The more affluent hotels had spoons designed for them. Many others simply had local craftsmen engrave spoon bowls with pictures of the hotel. These were sold in the ubiquitous hotel souvenir shops. In some cases, enterprising silver companies designed one spoon which pictured several hotels in a given area. These may have been sold by either the hotel souvenir shops or by local jewelers. Hotel spoons are fairly common. Spoons from some of the major affluent hotels are quite common, while spoons from smaller, relatively unknown hotels will be rarer. Price does not seem to be related to the rarity of any individual piece, however, but is based more on the aesthetic beauty of the individual piece. A collection of hotel spoons is very interesting.

Plate 625: Enameled, Cotton Palace, Charleston, S. Carolina; wavy handle; Shepard; $150.00 – 200.00.

Plate 626: Engraved, Hotel Colorad, Glenwood Springs, Colorado; LDA; $25.00 – 40.00.

Plate 625

Plate 626

Plate 627: Tampa Bay Hotel, Tampa Bay, Florida; black boy eating watermelon finial; Paye & Baker; $90.00 – 125.00.

Plate 628: Engraved, Coronado Tent City, San Diego, Calif.; Paye & Baker. (Note: Hotel Coronado in background. The tent city was a traditional camping area on the beach; rare; Hotel Coronado spoons are relatively common; there is also an embossed version of this spoon); $30.00 – 60.00.

Plate 629: Engraved, The New Elms, Excelsior Springs, Missouri; Virginia pattern, ca. 1910; Lunt; $30.00 – 50.00.

Plate 627

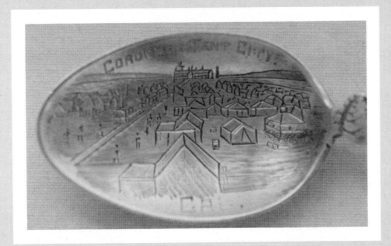

Plate 628

Plate 629

Plate 630: Postcard, Elms Hotel, Excelsior Springs, Mo.

Plate 631: Postcard, The Royal Poinciana Hotel, Palm Beach, Fla.

Plate 630

Plate 631

Plate 632: Top, engraved, Pine Grove Springs Hotel, Spofford, New Jersey; Newcastle pattern, ca. 1895; Gorham, $30.00 – 50.00; bottom, engraved, Royal Poinciana, Palm Beach, Florida; Orange pattern; Watson; $30.00 – 50.00.

Plate 633: Engraved, French Lick Springs Hotel, French Lick Springs, Indiana; Paye & Baker; $30.00 – 50.00.

Plate 634: Right, Engraved, Raymond Hotel, Pasadena, Calif.; Towle; Old English pattern, ca. 1892; $30.00 – 50.00; left, engraved, Raymond Hotel, Pasadena, Calif. (rebuilt after the fire of 1895). Note: The teddy bear finial; T. Roosevelt was a guest at the new hotel and the teddy bear was used to indicate this; $40.00 – 60.00.

Plate 632

Plate 634

Plate 633

Plate 635: Mount Lowe Railroad Incline, near Pasadena, Calif.; Wallace; $50.00 – 75.00; engraved, Echo Hotel, Pasadena; Coddington Bros.; enameled orange finial; $50.00 – 80.00; Great Cable incline, Mount Lowe; Shepard; $20.00 – 40.00; engraved, Alpine Tavern (top of Mt. Lowe), enameled mule (helped pull incline railroad for many years); prob. Shepard, #46, $50.00 – 70.00.

Plate 635

Plate 636: Engraved, Gayoso Hotel, Memphis, Tennessee; Watson; $30.00 – 50.00.

Plate 637: Engraved, Green Hotel, Pasadena, Calif.; LDA; $30.00 – 50.00; engraved, Green Hotel, Pasadena, Calif.; Shepard; $30.00 – 50.00.

Plate 636

Plate 637

— Military —

We find a number of different spoons relating to the military. Spoons honoring generals are frequently encountered. Full figurals showing generic uniforms are usually quite interesting and very detailed. Rifle spoons are also very collectible and are unusual.

The Spanish-American War occurred in 1898 when the spoon movement was quite popular. We find many spoons relating to this war even though it lasted only a few months. At the time it was a "popular war," but with 20-20 hindsight, many have determined that it is really a black mark on U.S. history. The basic cause of the war was a battle between the yellow journalism of Pulitzer and Hearst. Their stories about horrible incidents in Cuba were largely the result of the writers' imaginations. The U.S. sent the battleship *Maine* to Havana Harbor to investigate the charges. The battleship blew up. At first it was blamed on the Spanish, but later investigation indicated that it was probably a mechanical failure of the boiler. The Spanish offered reparations and tried conscientiously to avoid a war, but the "yellow journalists" inflamed the public. Teddy Roosevelt and his Rough Riders had a fairly easy victory over the Spanish in Cuba and Admiral Dewey had a very easy victory in Manila, Philippines. Both men became immediate heroes and we find spoons honoring them. The United States emerged from the war as a major world power and virtually ended Spanish hegemony in much of the world.

Plate 638: World War 1, U.S. Army; Robbins; $80.00 – 125.00; West Point Cadet; Watson; $ 80.00 – 125.00; World War 1, U.S. Navy; Robbins; $80.00 – 125.00.

Plate 639: Sir Walter Raleigh; no manuf. mark; $60.00 – 125.00; Spanish-American soldier; Watson; $60.00 – 125.00.

Plate 638

Plate 639

Plate 640: Engraved, <u>Maine</u>; Wallace; ca. 1898; $30.00 – 60.00.

Plate 641: Engraved, Battleship <u>Maine</u> USN, "blown up Feb. 13" (the final incident which started the Spanish-American War); $40.00 – 75.00.

Plate 642: West Point (Army training academy); enameled; custom-made, no manuf. mark; $30.00 – 50.00.

Plate 640

Plate 641

Plate 642

Plate 643: Engraved, <u>USS New York</u> (battleship); untraced; $30.00 – 50.00.

Plate 644: Acid etched bowl, Peekskill Military Academy, Peekskill, New York; $20.00 – 30.00.

Plate 645: Embossed bowl, Oliver Hazard Perry (helped defeat the British navy in the War of 1812); R. Lunt; $15.00 – 25.00.

Plate 643

Plate 644

Plate 645

Plate 646: Revolutionary soldier; Dominick; $45.00 – 75.00.

Plate 647: Anglo-Boer War, no manuf. mark; prob. American; $75.00 – 125.00; rifle; no manuf. mark; $50.00 – 75.00; rifle; F.E. Ladd; $ 50.00 – 75.00.

Plate 648: Rifle, Lucille Webb Banks, designer; $50.00 – 75.00; rifle, Minuteman, no manuf. mark; $50.00 – 75.00.

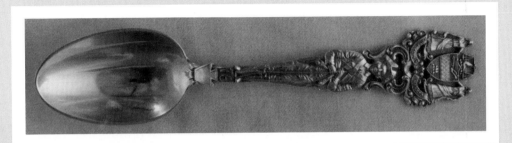

Plate 646

Plate 647

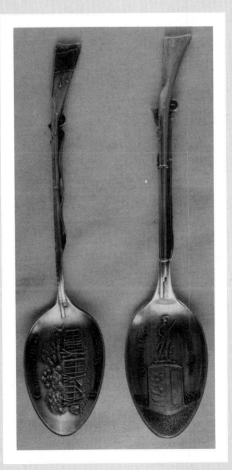

Plate 648

Plate 649: Confederate soldier; Gettysburg; Alvin; $60.00 – 80.00.

Plate 650: Soldier; Manchester/Baker; $60.00 – 80.00.

Plate 651: General (President) Jackson, Battle of New Orleans, "Old Hickory;" A.M. Hill 1891; $75.00 – 125.00; Confederate rifle; Mermod; $100.00 – 125.00.

Plate 649

Plate 650

Plate 651

— Advertising and Novelty Spoons —

Advertising products for increased sales has been a necessity for a long time. The adage, "if you build a better mousetrap, people will beat a path to your door" is simply not true. Even a product that we take for granted, such as natural gas, once was new and innovative and it was necessary to advertise its virtues.

The use of spoons to advertise products or locations was an important development in the new field of specialty advertising. Once this innovative use proved that it worked, other innovative types of advertising were tried.

Collectors of advertising spoons derive pleasure in studying the types of products that were produced and they also give us further insight into the common man's way of life. Most of these spoons are silver-plated although a few sterling ones are available. Prices can vary quite widely. Sometimes advertising spoons are not obvious to the casual observer. A few of the more interesting spoons are presented here.

Novelty figures have been placed on spoons since the beginning of the century. Most of the spoons with these figures are not sterling and many are not even silver-plated. Many of these pieces were advertising in nature, but some would also properly be considered souvenir spoons.

Children's spoons are collected by many people and they form an interesting display. Several manufacturers had complete lines of children's spoons and feeders. Furthermore they are relatively inexpensive and easy to find.

Plate 652: 5th St. store, Los Angeles; bowl embossed San Gabriel Mission; silverplate; no manuf. mark; $5.00 – 15.00.

Plate 653: Heinz; long handled pickle fork with pickle pin; silverplate; $20.00 – 50.00.

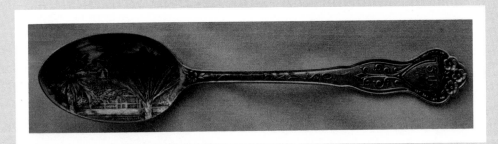

Plate 652

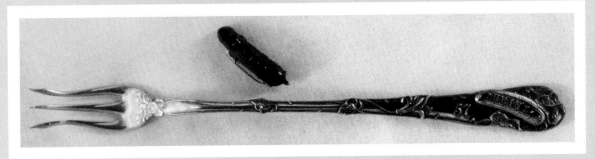

Plate 653

Plate 654: Kewpie, Rose O'Neill, enameled bowl; sterling; $100.00 – 150.00.

Plate 655: Woody Woodpecker, silverplate; IS; $5.00 – 15.00; Huckleberry Hound, silverplate, IS, $5 – 15; Dennis the Menace; silverplate; IS; $5.00 – 15.00; Betty Lou Carlton; silverplate; IS; $5.00 – 15.00.

Plate 656: Tony the Tiger; silverplate; IS; $5.00 – 15.00; Oh Oh Spaghettios; silverplate; IS; $5.00 – 15.00; Yogi Bear; silverplate; IS; $5.00 – 15.00.

Plate 654

Plate 655

Plate 656

Plate 657: Kewpie, bowl acid etched, "Taking baby to the circus;" sterling; Paye & Baker; $65.00 – 80.00.

Plate 658: Kewpie, detail; sterling; Paye & Baker.

Plate 659: Mickey Mouse; silverplate; Branford; $5.00 – 15.00; Donald Duck fork; stainless steel; ©Walt Disney; $5.00 – 10.00; Micky Mouse; stainless steel; ©Walt Disney; $5.00 – 10.00.

Plate 660: "Get the Habit — Cook with Gas;" sterling; $40.00 – 75.00.

Plate 657

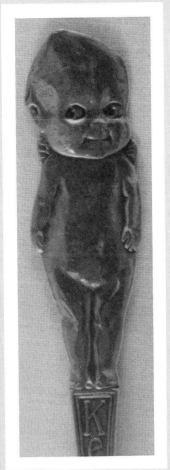

Plate 660

Plate 659

Plate 658

Plate 661: Pintsch, (gas lighting for American rail road cars); sterling; Alvin; $50.00 – 100.00; Northern Pacific, "Route of the great big baked potato," silverplate; Wallace; $10.00 – 20.00.

Plate 662: Pinocchio; silverplate; Duchess; $5.00 – 15.00; Howdy Doody; silverplate; Kagran; $5.00 – 20.00; Nestlé Quik; stainless; Imperial, Korea; $5.00 – 15.00.

Plate 663: Gerber; silverplate; Winthrop; $5.00 – 10.00; Gerber; silverplate; IS; $5.00 – 10.00; Gerber; Oneida; silverplate; $5.00 – 10.00.

Plate 661

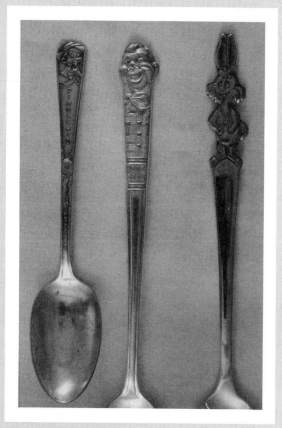

Plate 662

Plate 663

Plate 664: Banner Buggies; silverplate; Rogers; $10.00 – 20.00 each.

Plate 665: Dennis the Menace; silverplate; Dairy Queen; $5.00 – 15.00; Buster Brown; extra coin silverplate, $5.00 – 15.00.

Plate 666: Campbell Kids; silverplate; $5.00 – 10.00 each.

Plate 667: Charlie McCarthy; silverplate; Duchess; $5.00 – 20.00 each.

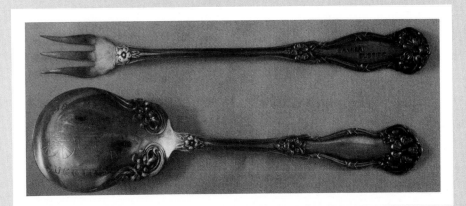

Plate 664

Plate 665

Plate 666

Plate 667

Plate 668: "See that Hump" – "hook and eye" (sewing advertising); silverplate; $5.00 – 15.00; Hershey; silverplate; IS; $5.00 – 10.00; Baker Chocolate; silverplate; $10.00 – 20.00.

Plate 669: Knox sparkling gelatin; silverplate; $5.00 – 10.00; Larkin, "Factory to Family," (soap distributor); silverplate; $5.00 – 15.00; Orient bicycles; silverplate; Alvin and Waltham Mfg.; $15.00 – 30.00.

Plate 668

Plate 669

Plate 670: Poland Water; sterling; Durgin; $40.00 – 75.00.

Plate 671: Round oak stove, Doewah Jack finial; silverplate; Childs & Co.; $10.00 – 30.00; Furniture City, Grand Rapids, Mich.; silverplate; Watson; $10.00 – 25.00; Towle log cabin; silverplate; $3.00 – 10.00.

Plate 672: Towle log cabin; silverplate; $3.00 – 10.00; Mr. Peanut; silverplate; $5.00 – 20.00; Heinz; silverplate; $5.00 – 15.00.

Plate 670

Plate 671

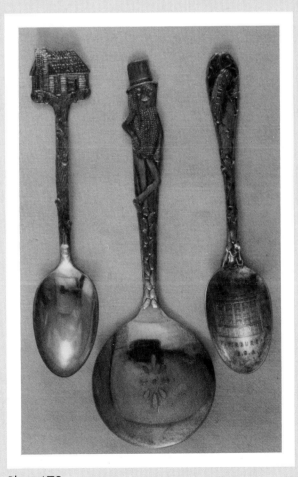

Plate 672

Plate 673: Billiken; sterling; Paye & Baker; (see more billikens under Alaska); $50.00 – 75.00.

Plate 674: Mary Poppins; silverplate; Roger Bros.; $5.00 – 15.00; Mary Poppins; silverplate; Walt Disney Prod.; $10.00 – 20.00.

Plate 675: Little Orphan Annie and dog; stainless steel; Korea; $10.00 – 15.00 each.

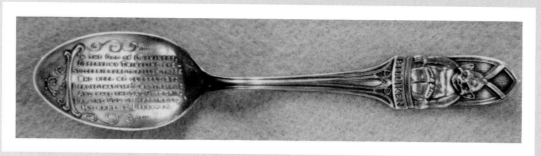

Plate 673

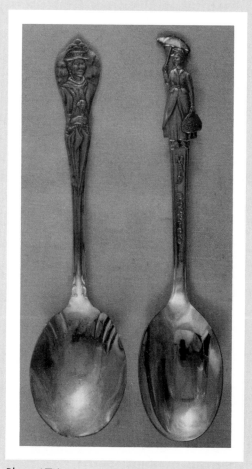

Plate 674

Plate 675

Plate 676: Heinz, with sample pickle pins; silverplate; $10.00 – 25.00.

Plate 677: Sorority Chocolates; silverplate; Rogers; $5.00 – 15.00 each

Plate 678: Buggies, (advertising spoon); silverplate; Roger Bros.; $10.00 – 25.00.

Plate 679: Las Vegas showgirl; unknown metal, not sterling; $3.00 – 7.00.

Plate 676

Plate 677

Plate 678

Plate 679

Plate 680: Cancer, June; Gorham, pat. 1894; $30.00 – 50.00. Aquarius, January; Gorham; $30.00 – 50.00.

Plate 681: Complete set of 12 Watson zodiac spoons; $150.00 – 225.00 ($10.00 – 20.00 each).

Plate 680

Plate 681

Note: Spoons are available for all symbols and all months.

Plate 682: Watson and Newell Co. catalog, ca. 1900 –1910.

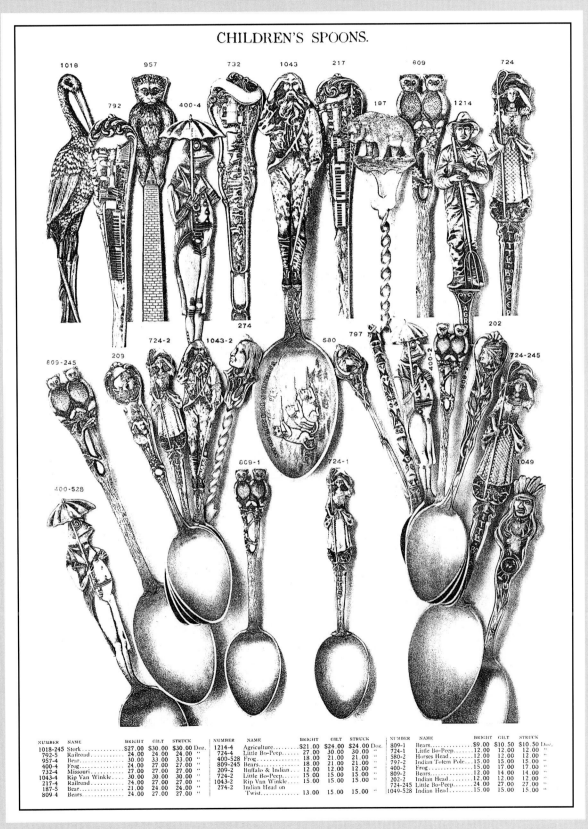

CHILDREN'S SPOONS.

NUMBER	NAME	BRIGHT	GILT	STRUCK		NUMBER	NAME	BRIGHT	GILT	STRUCK		NUMBER	NAME	BRIGHT	GILT	STRUCK
1018-245	Stork	$27.00	$30.00	$30.00	Doz.	1214-4	Agriculture	$21.00	$24.00	$24.00	Doz.	809-1	Bears	$9.00	$10.50	$10.50	Doz.
792-5	Railroad	24.00	24.00	24.00	"	724-4	Little Bo-Peep	27.00	30.00	30.00	"	724-1	Little Bo-Peep	12.00	12.00	12.00	"
957-4	Bear	30.00	33.00	33.00	"	400-528	Frog	18.00	21.00	21.00	"	580-2	Horses Head	12.00	12.00	12.00	"
400-4	Frog	24.00	27.00	27.00	"	809-245	Bears	18.00	21.00	21.00	"	797-2	Indian Totem Pole	15.00	15.00	15.00	"
732-4	Missouri	27.00	27.00	27.00	"	209-2	Buffalo & Indian	12.00	12.00	12.00	"	400-2	Frog	15.00	17.00	17.00	"
1043-4	Rip Van Winkle	30.00	30.00	30.00	"	724-2	Little Bo-Peep	15.00	15.00	15.00	"	809-2	Bears	12.00	14.00	14.00	"
217-4	Railroad	24.00	27.00	27.00	"	1043-2	Rip Van Winkle	15.00	15.00	15.00	"	202-2	Indian Head	12.00	12.00	12.00	"
187-5	Bear	21.00	24.00	24.00	"	274-2	Indian Head on					724-245	Little Bo-Peep	24.00	27.00	27.00	"
809-4	Bears	24.00	27.00	27.00	"		Twist	13.00	15.00	15.00	"	1049-528	Indian Head	15.00	15.00	15.00	"

Plate 682

Plate 683: Watson and Newell Co. catalog, ca. 1900 –1910.

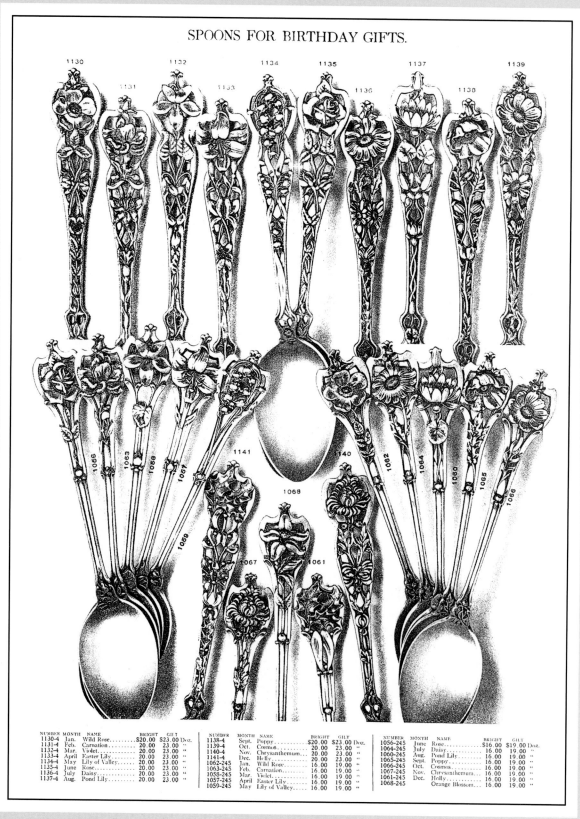

Plate 683

Plate 684: Watson and Newell Co. catalog, ca. 1900 –1910.

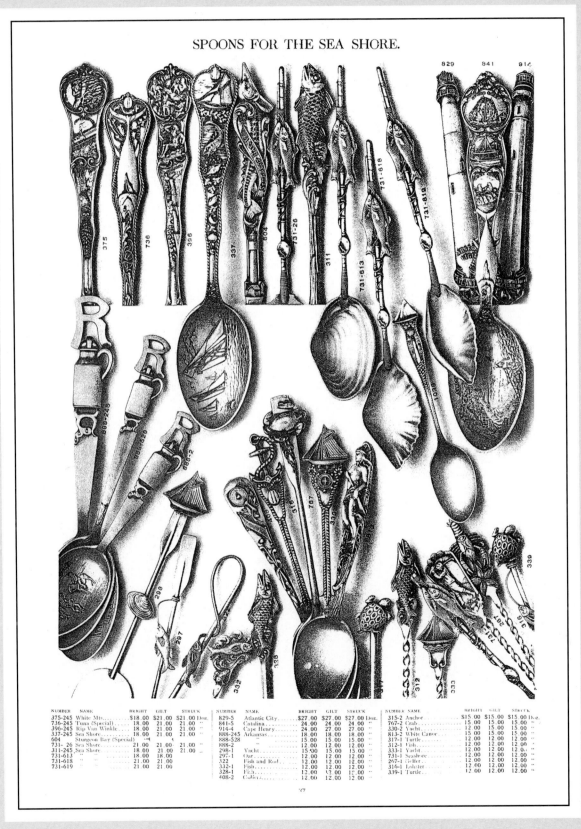

SPOONS FOR THE SEA SHORE.

Plate 684

273

Our Bowl Overfloweth

When I was first learning about spoons and silver, I kept asking people, how was this made? how do you know if this piece were made by a machine or by hand? how does a drop machine work? and dozens of other questions. Most of the time, knowledgeable dealers shrugged their shoulders and simply said, "I don't know." Sometimes dealers would say, "I've been doing this a long time and I can just tell," but they couldn't give me specifics and couldn't or wouldn't teach me how to do it myself. It was frustrating! Eventually I did figure it out. Like the long-term experts, I also learned to identify many pieces simply by looking at them. But part of the reason for writing this tome is to teach. Therefore, in the next few chapters I offer you specifics to look for. Some of this goes beyond the matter of spoons but applies to most silver items. Obviously I cannot make you an expert on old or historic silver in a few chapters, but hopefully I can guide you in the proper direction.

There are eight basic ways to create a picture on a spoon bowl. First is the use of a die stamp, second is individual engraving of a picture, third is an acid etching (sometimes called acid engraving), fourth is repoussé, fifth is enameling, sixth is transfer printing, seventh is casting, and eighth is painting.

The use of a die stamp (embossing) is the most common method. A designer will usually design the pattern or picture, then the tool and die maker will carefully translate the reverse of that pattern/picture into a steel block (the die). This translation requires minimal creative artistic abilities, but it is a difficult, time-consuming, and expensive job. Once the die is completed, it can be used repeatedly by semi-skilled personnel and is very cost effective. A piece of silver is placed between a steel backing plate and the steel die. A huge multi-ton drop press machine is used to press the silver into the die under extremely high pressure. There are a number of versions of this machine, but basically either hydraulic power or gravity is used to apply tremendous pressure to the silver. Since the silver metal is softer than the steel, the silver will conform to the shape of the picture in the die. This is basically the same method which is used to make coins. Each die can be used to make thousands of impressions and the result of each use is virtually identical. This is by far the best method for making copies of the same spoon or any relatively flat metal object. Ninety-eight percent of flatware handles are made with dies and 90%+ of the souvenir spoon bowls are made with dies. The easiest way to determine if a bowl picture is made with a die stamp is by feel. If the pattern is raised from the background and detailed, it was made with a die stamp. With practice you can usually determine this by eye alone (Plate 685). New Union Station is made with a die stamp because they expected to sell many spoons. As you can see, it produces a nice very detailed effect, but it usually lacks spontaneity and individuality. Plate 686 is an example of several scenes from a city.

Plate 685

Plate 686

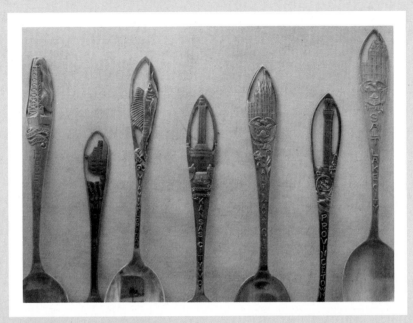

Plate 687

This image is also made using a die stamp. Because the process to create a die is rather expensive, it is necessary for the manufacturer to make and sell many pieces to justify the initial expense. Consequently there is generally less rarity among die stamp produced spoons. Separate dies are used for the handle and the bowl, thus it is not unusual to see the same bowl picture with different handles or vice versa. Some pieces are subjected to more than two dies depending on the effect the manufacturer wishes to create. For spoons which have cut-outs, a very sharp piece of steel is incorporated into the die or a separate cutout die is made (Plate 687). Double dies are used to create pictures or designs on the front and back of the handle at the same time.

The next type of spoon bowl is the hand-engraved pictures which you have seen repeatedly in this book. Less than nine percent of the souvenir type spoons will be hand-engraved since the making of this bowl is highly skilled, labor intensive, and much more expensive. For more information about engraving see the following chapter. Plate 688 shows similar San Francisco scenes. The top one is engraved and the bottom is produced by a die stamp and acid etched lettering. The first is an original work of art and the second is the product of a machine operation which is readily repeatable. The saleability of this scene was determined by the engraved pieces and thus the manufacturer decided to invest in the die creation process. For several reasons, embossed spoons make better photographs than hand engraved ones.

A third and uncommon method of creating a spoon bowl picture is by acid etching. A spoon bowl is first painted with a white paint. A picture is then drawn on it either freehand or traced or with a special transfer process. An awl is used which cuts through the paint, slightly scratching the metal. The white paint is then washed away and all parts of the picture which are not to be etched are covered with black asphaltum varnish, a chemical that will not be affected by acid. The acid (various types and concentrations are used) is then applied, and all exposed metal is eaten

Plate 688

Plate 689

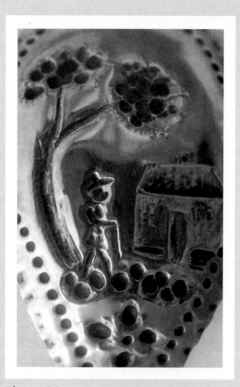

Plate 690

Plate 691

away. When the correct depth is reached (usually about ⅟₃₂"), the piece is washed in water to stop the etching process. Multiple copies of the same picture can be made using this method, but it is very difficult on a concave surface and the result is not as nice as the other methods. The Chicago Auditorium is an example of acid etching (Plate 689).

A fourth method is repoussé. In repoussé, the back of the metal is indented to cause the metal to bulge in the front. Then by using the skills of the engraver and chaser, the front is detailed to form a high relief picture. I have not found any American commemorative spoons using this process so to show the method I have used a Dutch Marriage spoon, ca. 1850 – 1875. Plate 690 shows how the metal is indented from the back and the enlarged version shows the different types of tool marks. Plate 691 is the front of the spoon. Additional chasing is required to improve the image quality. This process is even more time consuming than any of the others and is highly skilled and labor intensive. A silversmith must spend many years learning this skill.

There are machine variations which create a similar effect, such as Plate 692, a silver-plated Dutch example of the Liberty Bell. The lower portion of the die protrudes and raises the image. It can be very difficult to determine whether this type of piece is made by hand or machine except the machine-made ones usually are very detailed pictures and the handmade pieces tend to be not as detailed. If the piece is silver-plated, it certainly was made by machine. Experience in seeing many pieces is important here. Because of the large expense in creating this type of die, a lot of pieces must be made to justify the expense. If you see the same image on multiple pieces, you can be fairly certain that it was made by a machine.

The fifth method is enameling. Usually a very fine brush or spatula is used to paint a picture or design on the spoon bowl using a liquid enamel. After painting, the piece is fired in a kiln to chemically bind the enamel to the silver.

The sixth method is transfer printing (Plate 693). This is basically a simplified method of printing on metal and sometimes a picture is simply printed on paper and then glued to the metal. There is virtually no skilled activity involved and spoons, porcelain, ceramics or other objects can be made very cheaply. Sometimes examining the picture under a magnifying glass will show a regular pattern of black or colored dots. These are from the print screen that was used to make the picture and it is a dead giveaway that the picture was printed and then glued onto the metal. More information on this method is in the chapter on painted silver.

The seventh method is casting. Casting is as old as the use of silver and can be used for virtually any type of object. In the lost wax method, a piece of wax is carved and shaped as desired. The wax is then inserted into a sand or silica molding material. This is then heated at very high temperatures which causes the mold material to harden and the wax to melt. The hardened mold now contains an empty hole which is the exact image of the shaped wax. Silver is then heated until it liquifies and using centrifugal force, it is injected into the mold. When the silver cools and hardens, the mold is broken and the piece of silver is now in the same form as the original shaped wax. Examining a cast piece under a magnifying glass will usually reveal pieces of metal which look like they were melted, which is exactly what happened. Casting was often done for high relief or complicated designs, but it uses a lot more silver than do other methods. It also lacks much of the strength of other manufacturing methods. A few U.S. souvenir spoon bowls were made using this method, but most examples are of European or Middle Eastern origin.

Plate 692

Plate 693

Some full figure spoon handles are cast and many of the three-dimensional finials on spoons are cast. Plates 694 through 696 are examples of Gorham cast round bowls, the most known variety of American cast bowl spoons.

It is not unusual for a spoon to be made using several different processes. I have seen spoon bowls with some acid etching, engraved letters with chasing, and a die stamp created picture. Cast pieces are often touched up by hand using conventional tools. Sometimes cast parts are soldered onto machine-made (die) handles. Variations are interesting and fun to study.

How do you identify a spoon which is entirely hand made from a machine-made spoon? This is a tough question and sometimes even the experts have been fooled. Because it is so difficult to tell the difference, the machine-made pieces have a significant advantage in the marketplace. They are cheaper to produce and sell and the average consumer cannot identify the higher handmade quality. First, machine made spoons tend to be thinner than their counterparts. They also tend to be the same thickness along most of the handle. The manmade handles tend to be thicker in those spots that will have a lot of stress. A machine-made bowl will be the same thickness over the whole bowl, whereas a hand hammered bowl will be thicker around the front edge (which receives more use) than in the back of the bowl. Because the machine-made spoons are from a thinner piece of metal, they also tend to be springier than a handmade piece which has been forged several times. Most of this discussion refers to the older silversmithing standards for handmade spoons. When referring to products of Native Americans, this discussion does not apply since they did not follow the dictates of the older silversmiths. Plate 697 is a close-up detail of the handle of two spoons. The spoon on the top is a machine-made die stamped handle from the mid-1890s. It is very typical of spoons of this vintage and was not selected for any specific reason. The handle on the bottom is a "trailing vine" pattern which is handmade and hand chased, ca. 1830. It is an excellent example of silversmithing and typical of pieces of this vintage. It is almost impossible from the picture to determine which is the handmade piece. By actually holding the pieces and comparing them, assuming one has adequate knowledge, it is possible to determine, but it is still difficult. Since the average lay person wouldn't be able to make the determination, that lay person would not be willing to pay two or three times more for the better quality. This is one of the primary reasons that machine-made spoons have eclipsed handmade pieces.

Plate 694

Plate 695

Plate 696

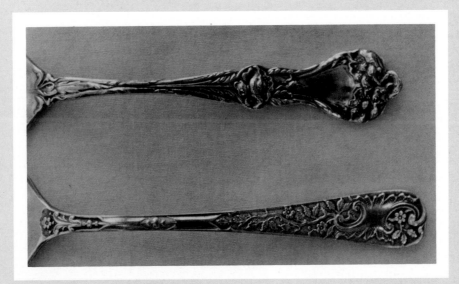

Plate 697

An Engraved Legacy

In this book we have shown numerous enlarged examples of hand engraving in spoon bowls. There have been more examples of these pieces than their actual percentage in the entire spoon population primarily because this author is intrigued and impressed by the quality of the workmanship and the designs.

First the engraver will make a sketch of the object on the spoon bowl either by drawing or by a transfer process. Then positioning himself next to a north-facing window (natural light is better than artificial light), he will very carefully use his graver tools to carve thin lines in the metal. As the graver cuts into the metal, a thin sliver of silver is removed. First the major lines of the picture are engraved; as it begins to take shape, smaller and smaller lines are cut into the metal to fill in the details. All the little cuttings are saved and melted for reuse. The engraver must continually sharpen his tools to ensure smooth lines. Considerable pressure must be placed on the graver tool, but the engraver must ensure that the cut is not so deep to cause gouges or so shallow to allow the tool to slip and scratch the metal in unwanted ways. This is a much tougher task than it sounds and the concave shape of a spoon bowl increases the problems. Sometimes the tool itself will break and cause unsightly problems. If you examine some of the pictures, you can determine where the engraver had problems and how he made other shapes and lines to disguise the problem since it is extremely difficultt to erase a bad line. Normally an observer would be unaware of these slight mishaps, but these pictures have been enlarged, and the flaws are more obvious.

After the picture is completed, any lettering is done. Many of the names and dates which are engraved were done separately at the time of purchase. There were numerous styles of lettering popular at this time in history, ranging from basic block lettering to fancy script, and the engraver had to be familiar with all of them. Plates 699 through 703 show some of the more popular styles of lettering.

If you run your finger across an engraved bowl, you can feel the cuts in the metal; if the bowl has not been polished many times, you can still feel the roughness of the cuts. Some dealers believe that if they can feel the "jaggedness," then the engraving is not as old. This is only partially true as the number of polishings or use is what reduces roughness. If a three-hundred-year-old piece were polished only once, it would still feel jagged whereas if a modern piece were polished many times, it would feel smoother. There were styles of engraving in various time periods and sometimes a dealer will say that the style is from another time period. This is sometimes true as it was not unusual for a piece of silver to be modified or engraved at a later date. Generally we do not have

Plate 698

Plate 699

Plate 700

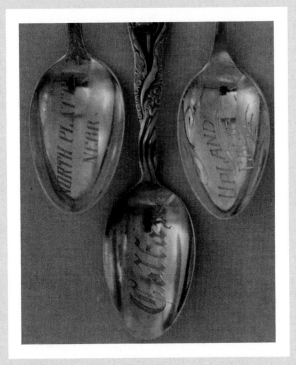

Plate 701

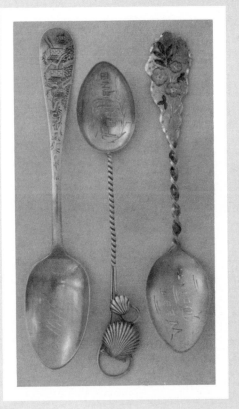

Plate 702

Plate 703

this problem with souvenir spoons and the dates and initials are from the time of purchase.

Some of the pictures were engraved at the factory and sometimes a local jeweler would hire a local engraver to do the work. The factory usually tried to get the jeweler to order a dozen images at the same time.

How long did it take to engrave a picture in the bowl of a spoon? The answer is not simple. Obviously a more complex picture would take longer and the more skilled an individual engraver, the faster he would be able to complete the work. If the engraver were doing multiple copies of the same design, later versions would be completed faster than the first versions. A consensus of opinion among dealers who have discussed this matter with me is that on average, a simple picture would take between three and four hours to engrave. More complex pictures might take six or more hours.

Plate 704 shows two pictures of engravings of the Minneapolis milling district. Both pieces have identical handles and were probably engraved by the same person. Close observation will reveal a number of small differences, including quality differences which are probably related to fatigue or time pressures. It is unusual to find pieces that can be identified as from the same batch and engraver. They are included here so you can see that as the engraver became familiar with a particular picture, changes were made. Most of these changes are subtle, but careful examination of the two pictures will reveal many minor differences.

Engraving is a highly skilled artistic activity. It takes about 10 years of practice to reach the master status. Most individual silversmiths did not do their own engraving, but contracted it out to specialists. Paul Revere was one of the few silversmiths who also did engraving on a professional basis. He is known to have engraved both silver items which he created and copper printing plates. The major silver manufacturers often had a few skilled engravers in their service, but these "artistic type" people did not fit well in an assembly line production. Management would often try various incentives to make them work faster and thus be more profitable, but records from Gorham and Tiffany indicate that such incentives usually did not work well. Most engraving is traditionally anonymous since it was usually subcontracted, but as an incentive both Tiffany and Gorham, for a time, allowed the engravers to mark their work. Some of the Gorham spoons pictured here which were engraved at the factory appear to be marked by the engraver on the back of the bowl (see Plate 705), but much research remains to be done.

Silver, copper, and steel engraving are basically the same process. Until the 1880s the printing industry employed most of the engravers to make plates for all their pictures. This was a highly paid skill passed along from generation to generation for hundreds of years. In the mid-nineteenth century the printing industry began experimenting with a new technique called lithography (literally, stone printing). Using this technique, the artist would draw the picture on a stone plate which would then be acid etched and used in the printing press. The very expensive and time-consuming step of engraving a steel (or copper) plate was eventually eliminated. The net effect of lithography was that picture printing became much easier and cheaper and thousands of highly-paid engraving jobs were eliminated. The famous firm of Currier and Ives was one of the American companies that led this technological revolution.

The silver industry was one of the few places a master artist-engraver could still find work after the printing industry's technological revolution no longer needed his services. Engraving had been used to enhance the look of silver for centuries. Most of the time silver objects were engraved only with names or initials and dates because of the difficulty and expense. In England some coat-of-arms

Plate 704

Plate 705

engraving was done on larger, more valuable pieces of silver. Picture engraving has been known since the 1500s but it was relatively expensive and therefore somewhat rare. We do find a few examples of picture engraving on various smaller pieces of silver including caddy spoons and small boxes from the first part of the nineteenth century but they are not overly plentiful. The American commemorative spoon revival, however, was a godsend to these engravers as it required extensive detailed work at relatively good wages. (The wages were not as good as those paid by the printing industry because there were more people applying for work than there were open positions.) The availability of skilled personnel created the opportunity to have limited-interest commemorative spoon bowl pictures hand-engraved without investing in the very expensive die creation process. If a jeweler needed one, five, or 10 commemorative pieces, it was simply not cost effective to have a die made, thus the engraved bowl was a natural substitute. Eventually the commemorative spoon revival ran its course and the public was no longer willing to pay the price for high quality hand engraving. Since there was virtually no further demand for engravers in any other industry, most of those highly trained people were forced to seek other lines of work. Needless to say, they did not pass on their skills to their children, and today we find no commercial engravers who are capable of doing the quality of work shown in this book.

A few people still retain the skill to do hand lettering without using a jig, but I have been unsuccessful in finding anyone who can do the picture work. If you would like to see an example of excellent modern day engraving, examine any denomination paper dollar in your wallet. American paper dollars are one of the very few items that are still made from engraved plates. Even the Bureau of Engraving which produces these plates is having an extremely difficult time finding capable engravers. They have had to start their own training process because they have been unable to hire skilled master engravers.

Plate 706 shows three pictures of the Masonic Hall in Chicago. All three show the same building and viewing angle but were most likely produced by different engravers. Examine them carefully. They are different and those differences show the artistry which is involved in engraving.

A variation on the engraving process is bright-cut engraving. To create this effect, the engraver uses a specially shaped scauper to remove a sliver of metal. This scauper creates tiny facets in the metal that shine brightly. You can see this effect in many of the pictures. Notice how the windows of the buildings are

Plate 706

brighter as if the lights were on. Sometimes the outlines of the buildings are also done with bright cuts. Bright-cutting is a more difficult technique but it was quite popular at this point in history. Sometimes an engraver will overuse the technique and some of the pictures show excessive bright-cutting. A skilled engraver is a true artist and you will see much variation depending upon each individual's skills.

Chasing and engraving are similar skills and we occasionally find some chased pictures in spoon bowls. In chasing, the metal is indented to form a design, whereas in engraving a sliver of metal is removed. The effect is different, but one has to examine the item very carefully with a magnifying glass to determine which process was used. In some cases the two skills are combined. In many pictures, trees and other foliage are done by chasing, whereas the main building is done by engraving. Chasing tends to promote the buildup of tarnish and is harder to clean.

Craftsmanship

— Art Nouveau and Art Deco —

Art Nouveau and Art Deco were two major artistic trends that had a very profound influence on silver manufacturing. Entire volumes have been written about each of these styles and there are books on silver which have also specialized in the effect of these styles.

Art Nouveau is primarily known for its very natural, sensuous women and curvy, flowery style. There were a number of spoons made in this style and the ones with nudes are very popular. In flatware design we find many variations and interpretations of the flowing, sensual curves which were very popular.

Art Deco is primarily known for a more stately linear style, but as the influence of this movement lasted a very long time, multiple flatware and souvenir spoons were created in this style. The souvenir spoon revival of the 1920s is particularly known for its Art Deco elements.

Eventually this movement gave way to Modernism. By this time silver was no longer considered essential to the household and only a few flatware styles were produced. Souvenir spoons in sterling silver were not being made in modernism, except by hobbyists.

Plate 707: Pretty lady; Towle, ca. 1910; $25.00 – 50.00.

Plate 707

Plate 708: Art Nouveau style.

Plate 709: Enameled, apple picker; J. Mayer Bros.; $150.00 – 250.00.

Plate 708

Plate 709

Plate 710: "Bacchante;" Mechanics; $75.00 – 125.00; grape picker; Fessenden; $100.00 – 175.00.

Plate 711: The Four Seasons; Mechanics also manufactured for Mermod Jacquard; $150.00 – 200.00 each, complete set $1,000.00+.

Plate 712: Reverse of Plate 711.

Plate 710

Plate 711

Plate 712

Plate 713: Detail; Atlantic City; no manuf. mark; $100.00 – 150.00.

Plate 714: Art Nouveau, engraved, "Clyde;" Paye & Baker; $40.00 – 75.00; sensuous nude, engraved Union Depot; Manchester/Baker; $50.00 – 90.00; engraved, "Milwaukee;" no manuf. mark; $30.00 – 70.00.

Plate 715: "Draped Figure;" Mechanics; $100.00 – 200.00.

Plate 716: Reverse of Plate 715.

Plate 713

Plate 714

Plate 715

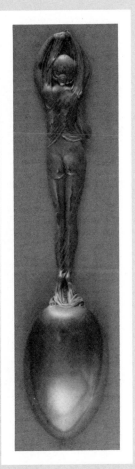

Plate 716

Plate 717: "Orange Goddess," J. Meyer Bros.; $200.00 – 300.00.

Plate 718: Mardi Gras, New Orleans; Fessenden; $75.00 – 150.00; apple picker; J. Meyer Bros., $100.00 – 200.00; draped figure; Shepard; plain bowl; $50.00 – 75.00.

Plate 719: Same handle as spoon in Plate 714, Mission San Buena Ventura embossed in bowl; Paye & Baker; $60.00 – 120.00; slightly smaller version; note cut-outs in handle around head and waist; Paye & Baker; $50.00 – 110.00.

Plate 717

Plate 718

Plate 719

Plate 720: Love Disarmed; depending on implement end; Reed and Barton; $150.00 – 300.00.

Plate 721: Art Deco style lady holding Canadian shield; no manuf. mark; $40.00 – 75.00; holding Colorado shield; no manuf. mark; $50.00 – 75.00; Holding St. Louis shield; Mermod Jacquard; $50.00 – 100.00.

Plate 722: Mermaid, Church of Guadalupe, Mexico; (available in several styles); Paye & Baker; $40.00 – 75.00; Golden Gate Exposition; silver-plated; $20.00 – 40.00; Fessenden; $30.00 – 50.00.

Plate 720

Plate 721

Plate 722

Plate 723: Full figural, dated 1871 in bowl (but this spoon was not produced at that time so the date must refer to something else); Larsen & Co.; $75.00 – 125.00.

Plate 724: Holding empty shield, smaller size; Hirsch & Oppenheimer; $40.00 – 80.00; larger size; Hirsch & Oppenheimer, $50.00 – 90.00. (Some are customized in the shield and bowl.)

Plate 725: Letter openers; Mechanics; $60.00 – 75.00; Durgin; $60.00 – 75.00.

Plate 725

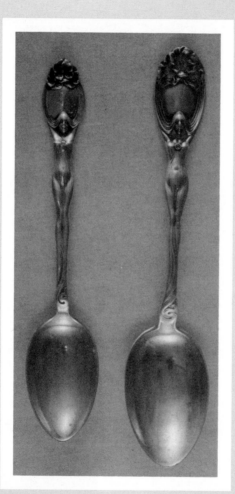

Plate 724

Plate 723

Plate 726: Watson and Newell Co. catalog, ca. 1900 – 1910.

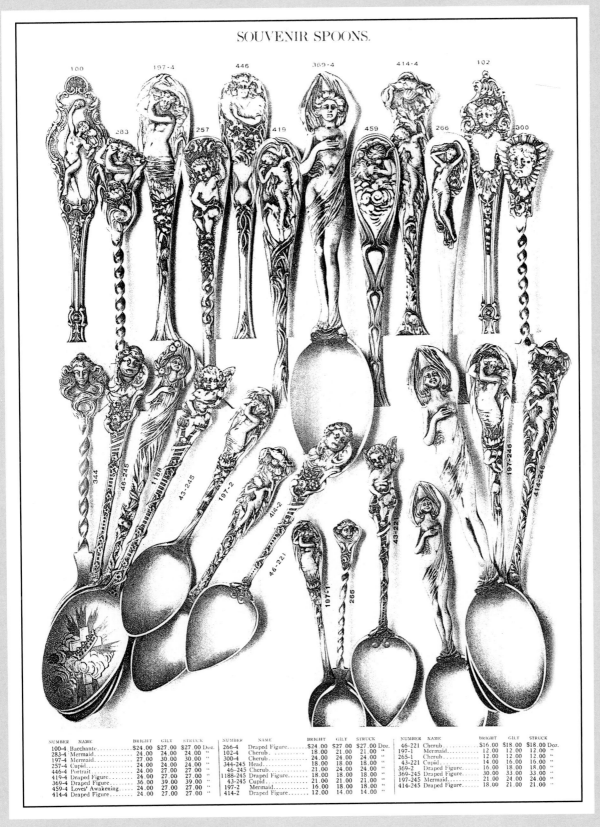

Plate 726

291

— Flatware Styles —

There was gradual change in the styles of silver flatware as manufacturers tried to capture the latest ideas that would appeal to the public, thus creating greater sales. Manufacturers proceeded at different paces depending on their understanding of public desires. Hundreds of different styles were created and the following pictures give a brief overview of a continuing process.

These examples show a general range of patterns; the dates show the evolution of the designs. Any book of flatware patterns will show considerable overlap which is exactly what we would expect. Even today, 100 later, I still prefer the Art Nouveau styles, so we would expect buyers of silver at that time would sometimes choose traditional styles over the newer styles.

Plate 727: Shows three patterns that were popular in the 1870 – 1880 period. Note that all these patterns were repeated in souvenir spoons.

Plate 727

Plate 728: Shows three patterns that were popular in the 1880s. Again we have seen elements of all these repeated in souvenir spoons.

Plate 729: Shows five patterns that were popular just before the beginning of the souvenir spoon movement (late 1880s through early 1890s). The use of figures and flowers was repeated in many souvenir spoons. These Art Nouveau style handles show classic sensuous figures, curvy lines, flowers, and other naturalistic elements. Note: the Gorham "Versaille" pattern (example 1) is now being reproduced using the original molds.

Plate 728

Plate 729

293

Plate 730: Shows six classic Art Nouveau styles of flatware handles. Many of the engraved pictures and other souvenir style spoons use these flatware designs (middle 1890s).

Plate 731: Shows six hand-engraved bright-cut flower handles from the early to middle 1890s. Most of these spoons use the classic, plain, rounded top popularized by Gorham's Mothers pattern (each manufacturer had its own version). These bright-cut Art Nouveau flowers are classics and were used repeatedly in the souvenir spoon movement.

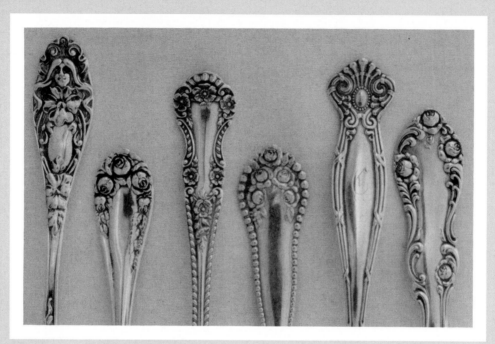

Plate 730

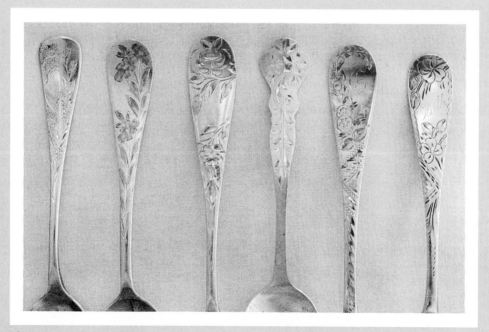

Plate 731

Plate 732: Shows four intermediate styles. Art Deco style was gradually making inroads into the public consciousness and the silver manufacturers were very eager to capitalize on the latest trends. While we still see some elements of Art Nouveau, the styles are becoming less complicated and more linear. (Late 1890s)

Plate 733: Shows classic Art Deco style flatware. We no longer have the curves and sinuous lines of Art Nouveau and have achieved a linear, sculptured style (after 1900). The souvenir spoon movement was slowing down at this point, but we still find a number of souvenir spoons which show Art Deco design elements. The souvenir spoon revival of the 1920s clearly shows these patterns.

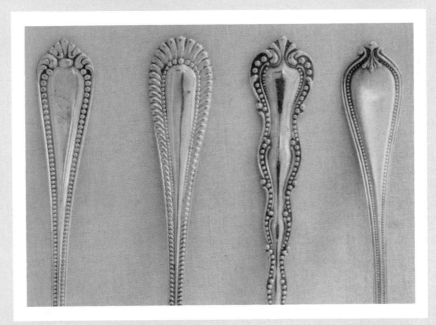

Plate 732

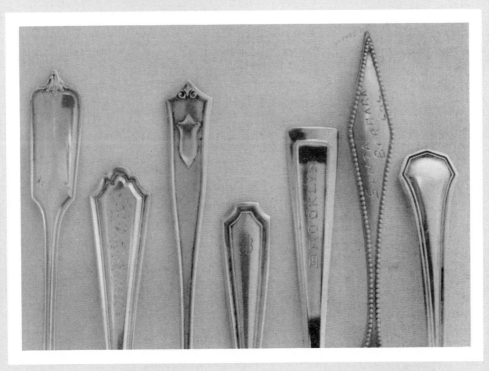

Plate 733

— The Arts and Crafts Movement —

The basic philosophy of the Arts and Crafts Movement is that purity in art purifies the soul. Ruskin and Morris believed the decorative arts were the catalyst to introduce art into everyday life. In the United States the Arts and Crafts movement coincided with the souvenir spoon movement (1890 – 1915) and champions such as Hubbard and Stickley, taught through the beauty of handmade furniture and decorative silver that their art restored the soul of the user and the maker. They believed that mass-produced items (such as machine-made souvenir spoons) destroyed the soul of both the maker and the user and were an abomination.

In a rejection of mass-produced silver, some American silversmiths "purified" their work and produced items of beauty and high practicality. Today in spoon collecting we can still find beautiful spoons that were the product of their individual maker's imagination. These spoons are handmade, one-of-a-kind, representing the virtues of hand craftmanship. Most of them are the work of hobbyists and "believers" as it was very difficult to earn a living following this philosophy.

But it was also very difficult for the average person to determine when a product was handmade or machine made. The machine product has a distinct advantage over the handmade product in that it looks very similar but is much cheaper. Arts and Crafts followers started to leave slight hammer marks in silver to show they were hand-pounded. About the time the public understood this technique, manufacturers supplied a similar product which was the product of an automatic hammer. The struggle between manufacturer and craftsman continued but as soon as the craftsman developed a market, a manufacturer found a way to produce a similar product for less money.

Some craftsmen adopted half-way measures to stay competitive. They would use machine-pressed bowls (very time consuming to make by hand), but handmade finials and stems. Some of these items are pictured. This defeated the basic philosophy of A & C, but allowed them to stay in business.

The basic concepts of Arts and Crafts exist in our own day and we often pay homage to them, but in most struggles between craftsmanship and machine, craftsmanship eventually loses, and Arts and Crafts is no exception. Even as I write this, the computer has defeated the Grand Master of chess in what is described as the ultimate test of human analysis.

Plate 734: Hawaiian dime, dated 1883, on twisted stem with engraved bowl; no mark; $100.00 – 125.00.

Plate 734

Note: The hand-engraved pictures in spoon bowls are still the work of craftsmen. No machine has yet been able to duplicate their quality or workmanship, but as we have repeatedly seen, the embossed bowls, which are the product of a machine, often command a higher price than the higher quality engraved pieces. This is the same problem faced by the A & C craftsmen at the turn of the century. Perhaps some day it will change.

Plate 735: Hand-pounded "austere style" fork; Allan Adler; Los Angeles, Calif.; $100.00 – 150.00.

Plate 736: Handmade applied leaf design; note the interesting bowl shapes; untraced mark; $50.00 – 75.00 each.

Plate 737: Very elegant hand-pounded salad set in Navajo style with beautiful inlaid turquoise cabochons; no manuf. mark; $100.00 – 150.00 set.

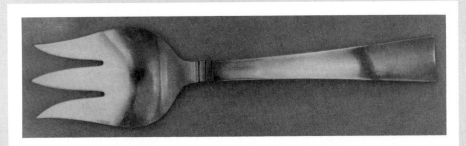

Plate 735

Plate 736

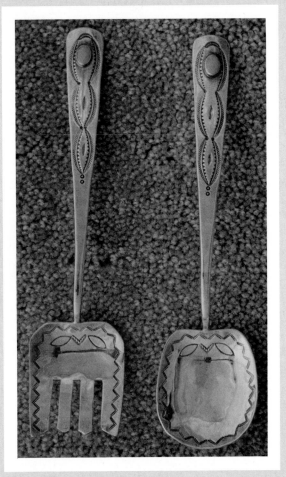

Plate 737

Plate 738: Handmade handle with applied flowers and acid etched, gold washed bowl; sterling; untraced manuf. mark; $25.00 – 50.00; cast and pounded finial and serrated handle; sterling; no manuf. mark; $20.00 – 50.00; cut-out and engraved finial on twist handle; heart-shaped bowl; sterling; no manuf. mark; $25.00 – 50.00; engraved finial with twist handle and heart-shaped bowl; sterling; no manuf. mark; $25.00 – 50.00.

Plate 739: U.S. nickel finial on double-twisted stem with a quarter-bowl, no mark; $100.00 – 150.00; Jerusalem cross on twisted handle with U.S. quarter-bowl (possibly made in Philippines); $75.00 – 125.00.

Plate 738

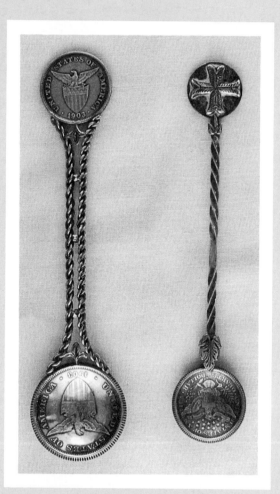

Plate 739

Plate 740: Enameled sword on shell-shaped bowl; sterling; $20.00 – 40.00; cut-out and serrated design on twist handle; sterling; $20.00 – 40.00; front engraved "Hutchinson," back engraved "Winnie age 6"; $20.00 – 40.00; cut-out engraved finial on twist handle; sterling; $20.00 – 40.00; cut-out finial on twist handle; sterling; $20.00 – 40.00.

Plate 741: Beautiful handmade sunflower; possibly Oriental; sterling; no manuf. mark; $50.00 – 100.00.

Plate 741

Plate 740

Plate 742: Cast fiddle, unmarked; $20.00 – 40.00; stamped flower finial on post, heart-shaped bowl engraved "Sarah;" $15.00 – 25.00; crowned spoon on hand-pounded stem and bowl; sterling; untraced mark; $20.00 – 40.00; applied flower finial on twisted stem and engraved picture "Lexington Mill," Butte, Montana; sterling; $30.00 – 50.00.

Plate 743: Very elegant and sophisticated hand-pounded ladle with a "B" finial; John O. Bellis, Calif., ca. 1910; believed to be for personal use; $50.00 – 100.00.

Plate 742

Plate 743

Plate 744: Hand-worked demitasse spoons; cut-out and engraved finial, twist handle, heart-shaped bowl; sterling; no manuf., mark; $20.00 – 50.00; knot twisted handle and finial, heart-shaped bowl; no marks; $20.00 – 40.00; cut-out and engraved, Columbus for 1893 Columbian World's Fair; sterling; $25.00 – 50.00; cut-out and engraved crescent on twist handle, heart-shaped bowl; sterling; $20.00 – 40.00; posy holder, twist handle; sterling; $20.00 – 50.00.

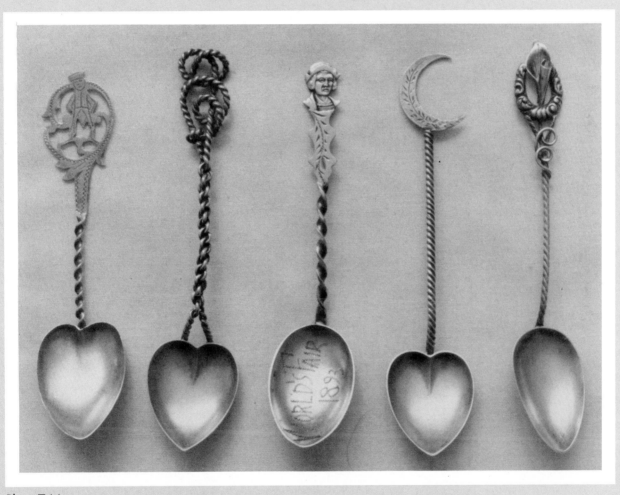

Plate 744

Plate 745: Custom cut-out of knight from a conventional spoon; no manuf. mark; back engraved "Will from Starr Aug. 22 '92." (A very interesting adaptation of a conventional plain-handled spoon); $40.00 – 75.00.

Plate 746: Antique head, "Arminius" from a series of 12 by the Sterling Company, Providence Rhode Island; designed by R. Bujanoff. S.F; $50.00 – 85.00.

Plate 747: Austere two prong ends on tongs; Leonore Doskow, New York, after 1934; $75.00 – 125.00.

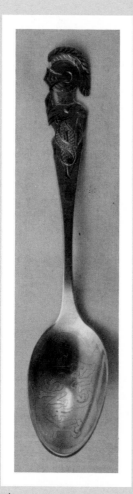

Plate 745

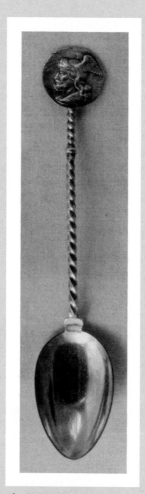

Plate 746

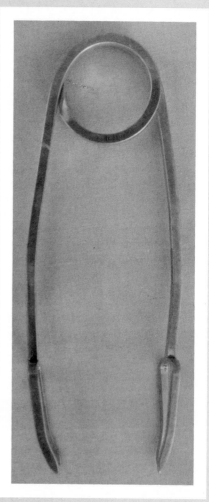

Plate 747

— Gemstones —

A distinctive class of spoons are those bearing gemstones. Semi-precious gemstones have been used since the beginning of history, and it was not uncommon to find them on silver and gold objects during the Middle Ages. Generally speaking they were not found on spoons, but the Arts and Crafts movement and the popularity of the flatware by the English firm of Liberty & Co. repopularized the use of gemstones on silver.

Most of the stones used are turquoise, but other semi-precious stones, shells, teeth, etc. can also be found. The American Indians of the Southwest made a number of these pieces, but most of their work is not marked as to purity or origin. One can only recognize their work from experience. The American Indian pieces will almost always have a distinctive type of engraving/hand stamping which becomes readily recognizable with experience.

Spoons with gemstones were also made in many other countries in even greater quantities and many of those pieces are also unmarked, so one should not assume that an unmarked piece is of American origin.

Spoons of this genre are very interesting and show nice workmanship, but the prices range very widely.

Plate 748: Round turquoise cabochon, sterling, untraced manuf.; $25.00 – 40.00; dark green cabochon (possibly jadeite); S. Kirk; $40.00 – 75.00; three round turquoise cabochons; sterling; untraced manuf.; $30.00 – 50.00.

Plate 749: Detail of turquoise cabochon on handmade Southwest Indian tea stirrer; $35.00 – 60.00; two gold nuggets, bowl engraved "Dawson" (Alaska – Yukon territory). (The story behind the terrible conditions that the miners encountered in their search for Alaskan gold is very interesting and well documented). $40.00 – 75.00.

Plate 748

Plate 749

Plate 750: Elk's tooth finial on a custom handle; Colorado Springs; no mark; $100.00 – 150.00.

Plate 751: Tiger eye agate handle on bowl with ears and engraved mule; Dadin; patented; $100.00 – 150.00.

Plate 752: Agate handle on bowl engraved "Denver;" no mark; $50.00 – 100.00; mule finial on twisted stem and agate bowl; sterling; $50.00 – 100.00.

Plate 753: Agate finial on dual twig stem; marked sterling and handmade; untraced manuf.; $50.00 – 100.00.

Plate 750

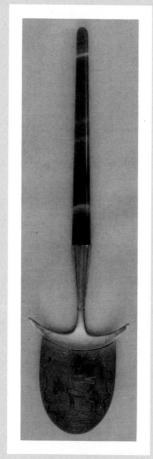

Plate 751

Plate 752

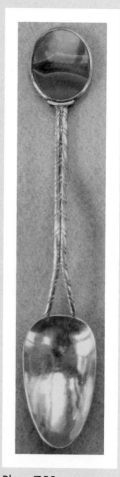

Plate 753

Plate 754: Petrified wood mounted to stem and engraved "petrified forest" in bowl; Tammen; $50.00 – 75.00.

Plate 755: Birthstone spoons with verse embossed in bowl, Sept., Jan., May, Feb.; Blackington; $40.00 – 75.00 each.

Plate 756: Moss agate finial on handmade spoon; believed to be Navajo; $40.00 – 90.00.

Plate 754

Plate 755

Plate 756

Plate 757: Assembled prospector spoon with turquoise in pan which is labeled "St. Louis;" the shovel-shaped bowl is marked "Porterfield Turquoise Mines, Silver City, New. Mex." (New Mexico); Mechanics; $60.00 – 120.00.

Plate 758: Detail of long-handled jeweled seafood fork; gold plated (not sterling); $10.00 – 25.00

Plate 759: Obsidian arrowhead finial with Mt. Hood engraved in bowl; unmarked; $50.00 – 75.00; quartz arrowhead finial with Mt. Hood engraved in bowl; sterling; $50.00 – 75.00.

Plate 760: White stone faceted like a diamond on flowered cut-out finial with twist handle; bowl engraved "Nannie;" sterling; demi; $30.00 – 70.00.

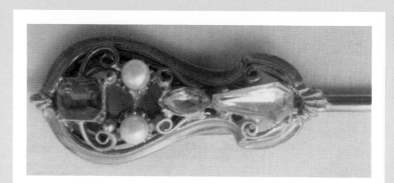

Plate 758

Plate 757

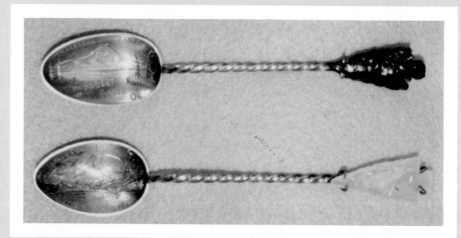

Plate 759

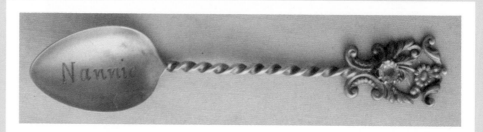

Plate 760

— Plique-à-jour —

Plique-à-jour is the rarest, most difficult, and prettiest of the various enamel processes. Liquid or powdered enamel is usually applied to a surface and then fired to melt and chemically bind it to the metal. In champlevé, the enamel is applied between two raised surfaces that were part of the original die stamping or casting. In cloissonné, the enamel is applied between cells which have been created by the application of thin wire to the surface of the object. But in plique-à-jour, there is no backing to the enamel. The cells must be kept small and the enamel is applied between the open cells and held in place by surface tension or a mica backing plate. After firing, the enamel becomes hardened and permanently attached to the sides. This is a very difficult process for even the most skilled artisans.

The net effect is that the enamel becomes translucent and light streaming through it creates a beautiful stained glass effect reminiscent of the stained glass windows in European cathedrals. Plique-à-jour spoons are truly miniature works of art.

All plique-à-jour pieces are custom-made and rare. Most pieces are less than 4" in length. Very little confirmed American-made plique-à-jour is to be found. The majority of the pieces are from France or the Scandinavian countries with some pieces from Austria, Russia, and China. It is even possible that some of the pieces shown here with American city names may have been produced in another country. Many pieces of plique-à-jour are not marked as to origin or metal content but they are almost always a good grade of silver or gold wash over silver. One should consider the quality of the workmanship and design and balance that against the asking price in making a purchase decision.

Plique-à-jour is also fragile and breaks relatively easily. Before buying any plique-à-jour piece, examine it carefully by holding it up to the light. If there are any empty cells, the value of the piece is radically reduced because it is very expensive to repair.

Obviously, special consideration should be given to the storage and display of these pieces to protect them from damage.

Even photographing plique-à-jour spoons is a challenge. To show the beauty of these pieces, it is necessary to have a pure light shining through the piece which means that light is flooding the camera with exposure problems.

Plique-à-jour spoons are rare and expensive for their size.

Plate 761: Pair of very similar plique-à-jour spoons with extensive workmanship in both the bowl and finial; sterling; maker not traced; possibly European; $100.00 – 150.00 each.

Plate 761

Plate 762: Interesting bowtie under colorful enamel; bowl engraved "Los Angeles;" sterling; no manuf. mark; $75.00 – 150.00.

Plate 763: Very interesting finial; sterling; no manuf. mark; back of bowl engraved "Denver;" $125.00 – 175.00.

Plate 764: Rare large serving spoon with extensive plique-à-jour work and unusual filigree in handle; sterling; Campbell Metcalf, Providence, Rhode Island; ca. 1892 – 98; $225.00 – 400.00.

Plate 765: Detail of serving spoon, Plate 764.

Plate 763

Plate 764

Plate 765

Plate 762

Plate 766: Pretty green finial design; sterling; bowl engraved "Kansas City;" no manuf. mark; $60.00 – 125.00.

Plate 767: Nice green leaf effect in bowl; sterling; bowl engraved "Denver"; Gorham #761; $100.00 – 150.00.

Plate 768: "Los Angeles" in plique-à-jour in bowl; sterling; no manuf. mark; $70.00 – 150.00.

Plate 769: "San Francisco" in plique-à-jour in bowl; sterling; no manuf. mark; $70.00 – 150.00.

Plate 770: Very pretty flower and leaf design with wire-wrapped stem; sterling; no manuf. mark; possibly European; $75.00 – 150.00.

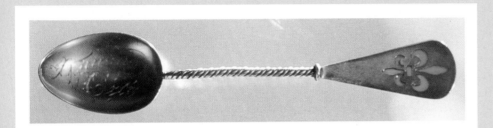

Plate 766

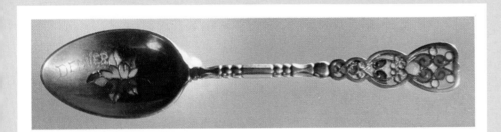

Plate 767

Plate 768

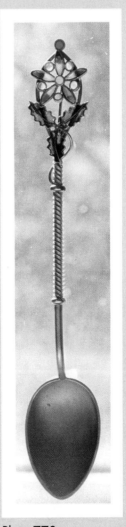

Plate 770

Plate 769

Plate 771: Beautiful stained glass effect in bowl and finial; Shiebler #5402; $150.00 – 400.00.

Plate 772: Small plique-à-jour design in finial; sterling; bowl engraved "Chicago;" no manuf. mark; $40.00 – 80.00.

Plate 773: Very nice serrated wire design; sterling; bowl engraved "San Antonio, Texas;" no manuf. mark; $40.00 – 75.00.

Plate 774: Nice flower design; sterling; bowl engraved "New York;" B& E (not traced); $40.00 – 75.00.

Plate 772

Plate 771

Plate 773

Plate 774

Note: A new "cold" enamel can be used to repair plique-à-jour. The repair is very difficult to detect if well done. The same chemical can be applied to filigree to create a similar effect. This new practice is being used commercially in Mexico. It is a low skilled activity. I have not yet seen it used on spoons, but I have seen it on silver filigree jewelry.

Painted Silver

Among the prettiest and most expensive of American spoons are those with pictures painted in the bowls. There are several ways of producing color pictures in spoon bowls and the alert collector/investor should learn the various techniques of determining which method was used before buying. To identify the manufacturing process, a magnifying glass of at least 10x power must be used. These pictures have been enlarged so a magnifying glass is not necessary.

A picture is painted freehand by a miniaturist. The painting is then covered with a clear protective untinted enamel glaze which is fired in a separate process. Each example of this type is a unique work of art and should be highly prized. On a painted bowl under magnification, you will see obvious brush strokes (usually oil paints) and will often see parts of the painting are heavier than others. You should not see a design in black. The objects are painted with the actual colors required. The result is only as good as the capability of the individual artist. This is a skilled operation and requires artistic talent. Plate 775, "Pride of Kentucky, Lexington," is a very fine rendition of a beautiful racehorse. The color variation in the lettering is a manufacturing defect that lessens the value slightly, but overall this is a well-done piece.

Opaque enamel is also used to create a picture or design. This is a less skilled operation and does not require significant artistic talent. A reasonably adept person can master the basic techniques with less than a week's training. The results are pretty but fairly mechanical. The opaque enamel (vitreous glass which has been ground to a powder) is evenly applied to the surface and then fired until it melts. Variations on this method include cloisonné where the indentations are made by the application of silver wire to the surface before the enamel is applied (very labor intensive and a highly skilled operation); champlevé is a cheaper, easier way to achieve a cloisonné effect. Some people and manufacturers often advertise it as cloisonné. Champlevé is a low-skilled activity whereas cloisonné is a very highly-skilled activity and the difference is difficult to detect. Cloisonné demands a higher price than does champlevé, $20 – 35, or true cloisonné, $100 – 150. Plate 776 shows champlevé where the indentations are put into the metal during the stamping process (low-skilled) and bassetaile where the metal is gouged out before the enamel is applied (a very old process). I have never seen bassetaile or cloisonné used on an American spoon, but have seen both used on spoons from other countries.

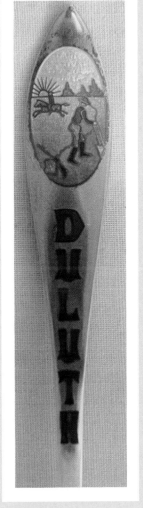

Plate 775

Plate 776

On the Vermont spoon (Plate 777), the red enamel is opaque and the picture is a hand-colored transfer print. Note the small missing chip at the left which reduces the value of the piece.

For transfer pictures, an outline is made by a miniaturist and then transfer printed onto the spoon bowl or finial (a similar method is used for glass and ceramic). Numerous copies of the same picture are easily made. The original outline is usually engraved on a hard surface, such as copper. Ink is applied to the surface and the excess is wiped up leaving ink in the indentations. A waxed paper is then laid across the inked surface and pressure is applied. The ink in the indentations is transferred to the paper which is then applied to the new spoon bowl, porcelain or other object and the ink is redeposited on the new surface. The transfer print is usually done in black and then hand colored. The hand coloring operation is very similar to a child's coloring book. The colorist is simply required to keep the color "between the lines." This method of creating colored pictures was used with great success by the printing firm of Currier and Ives and has been used on numerous objects over the intervening years. The colorist requires very little training. The result is pretty, but should not result in an artistic price.

It is very important for a prospective buyer to be able to determine when a spoon bowl is transfer printed and colored so as not to overpay. Under magnification, you will see the basic design in black and you will often see small black marks

Plate 777

throughout the design. The colors will appear like water colors which have been brushed over the black lines. Often you will observe that the colorist painted "outside the lines," or failed to fill in color between the lines. This is usually most obvious around trees and bushes but can also be observed on other parts of the design.

The majority of picture enamel bowl spoons and picture enamel finials use this process. The stagecoach and Indian figures in Plate 778 are transfer printed. The lettering is hand done. Note the coloring of the Indian, driver's shirt, and wheel of the coach. It is quite common to use the same pigment throughout the scene. Note the same blue for the mountains, coach windows, and bottom. Note on the rear coach wheel how the orangish color is outside the lines. Note at the grass how the color is just spread across the black marks. This is one of the better examples of hand coloring which I have seen. Plate 779 is a little easier to identify. Note the yellow color around the sun. The colorist made no attempt to keep it within the lines. Notice how the blue in the ocean is merely spread across the black lines which are supposed to represent waves. Notice how the central building is the same brown as the rocks across the bay and the ship has the same yellow color as the sun. Plate 780 readily shows the lines of the transfer print and the blue and green coloring in the leaves. Also note the blue wash on the right side which ignores the rest of the pattern. If in doubt, ask yourself if you were painting this picture, would you do it this way.

Modern color printed pictures, either halftone or four-color process, are glued into the spoon bowl and then covered with a protective lacquer layer. Virtually all modern souvenir spoons use this cheaper method. The result is a nice picture similar to that found in a magazine. It is not a skilled operation and should not command a premium price. Under magnification, you will see a regular pattern of either black dots or multicolored dots depending on the printing method used.

Plate 778

Plate 779

Plate 780

Note: If you examine the pictures in this book with a magnifying glass, you will see a regular pattern because these pictures were printed with a four-color or halftone process. Examination of the actual pieces or photographs will reveal the true details of workmanship used in the piece.

Plate 781: Watson and Newell Co. catalog, ca. 1900 – 1910.

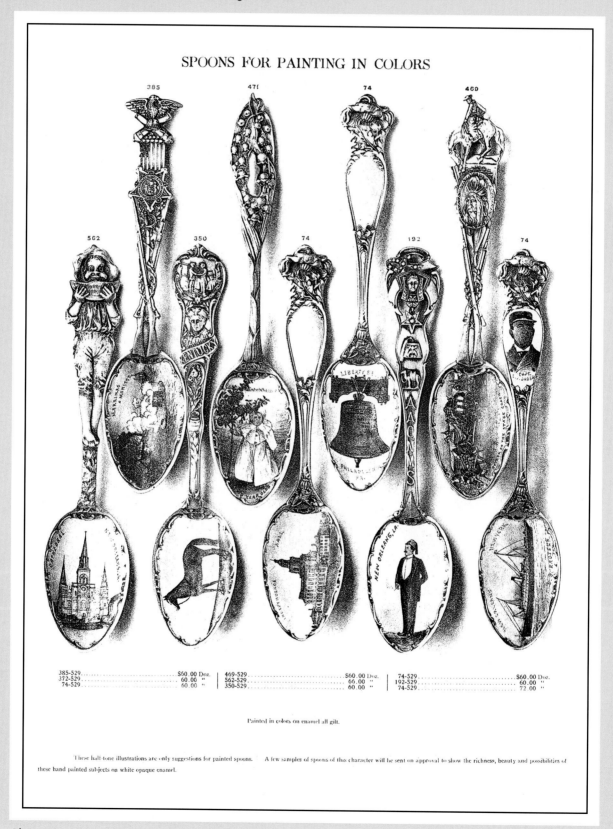

Plate 781

314

Plate 782: Watson and Newell Co. catalog, ca. 1900 – 1910.

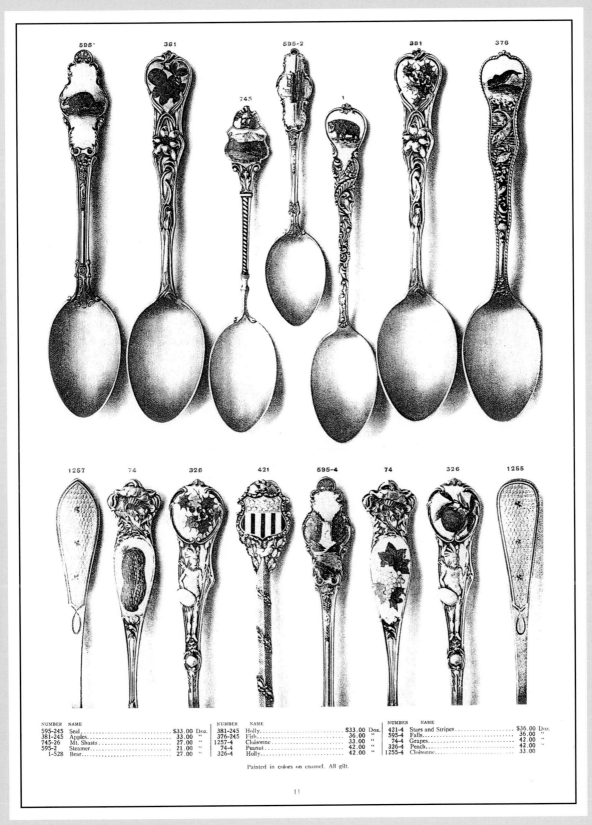

NUMBER	NAME		NUMBER	NAME		NUMBER	NAME	
595-245	Seal	$33.00 Doz.	381-245	Holly	$33.00 Doz.	421-4	Stars and Stripes	$36.00 Doz.
381-245	Apples	33.00 "	376-245	Fish	36.00 "	595-4	Falls	36.00 "
745-26	Mt. Shasta	27.00 "	1257-4	Cloisonne	33.00 "	74-4	Grapes	42.00 "
595-2	Steamer	21.00 "	74-4	Peanut	42.00 "	326-4	Peach	42.00 "
1-528	Bear	27.00 "	326-4	Holly	42.00 "	1255-4	Cloisonne	33.00 "

Painted in colors on enamel. All gilt.

11

Plate 782

315

Plate 783: Top: painted flag finial with engraved Statue of Liberty bowl; $40.00 – 75.00; bottom; painted flag finial with engraved hotel picture bowl; if perfect, $40.00 – 75.00, as is, $15.00 – 25.00.

Plate 784: Left: Indian figural handle with painted picture of Niagara Falls, N.Y.; $200.00 – 300.00; right ; Akahidala half-stem figural on column mount, enameled coat of arms bowl; $350.00 – 500.00.

Plate 785: Left: enameled figural of George Washington with plain bowl; $140.00 – 220.00; right: enameled stem with flag and Washington with the Capitol building impressed in bowl; $50.00 – 80.00.

Plate 783

Plate 784

Plate 785

Plate 786: Top: full figural alligator with transfer picture of the Seminole Indians canoeing down the Miami River; $150.00 – 225.00; Bottom: allegorical woman from San Francisco Pan Pacific Expo with painted picture of the famous San Francisco Cliff House in bowl; $150.00 – 275.00.

Plate 787: Top: Tennessee state handle with transfer print of a levee scene; $100.00 – 150.00; bottom: California state handle with painted orange flowers, from Redlands; (smudge lowers price) $125.00 – 175.00.

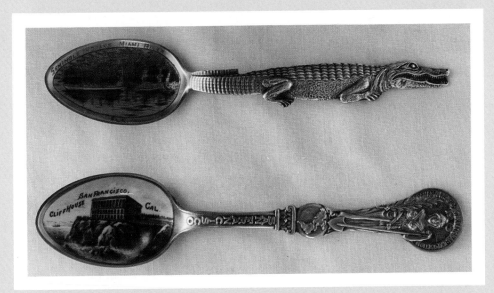

Plate 786

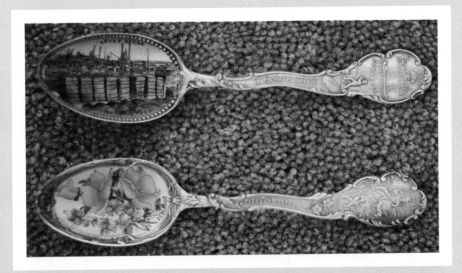

Plate 787

Plate 788: Top: Wisconsin state handle with transfer printed scene of the Wausau Fleet; $100.00 – 150.00; middle: Oregon state handle with transfer print of famous game bird bowl; (smudge lowers price) $100.00 – 150.00; bottom: Virginia state handle with painted picture of the Richmond State Capitol building; $125.00 – 225.00.

Plate 789: Close-up of transfer print of Wausau Fleet.

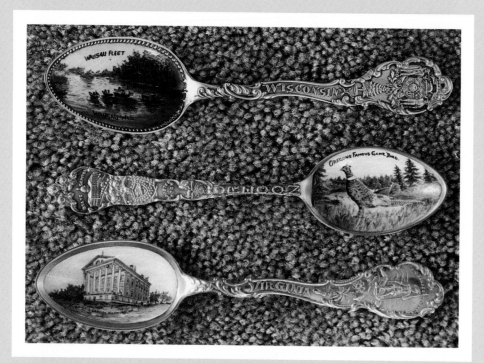

Plate 788

Plate 789

Plate 790: Left: flowered handle with transfer print and enameled bowl of Vermont; (light spot is a reflection of the camera lights); $100.00 – 150.00; middle: Army and Navy handle with painted American Flag bowl; $100.00 – 200.00; right: Nevada state handle with painted "Pride of the Desert" bowl; $150.00 – 275.00.

Plate 791: Left: City of Los Angeles handle with enameled flag bowl; $50.00 – 150.00; right: enameled Atlanta handle with enameled cotton flower bowl; $85.00 – 150.00.

Plate 790

Plate 791

Plate 792: Top: multi-scene California state handle with transfer print picture of poinsettias in bowl; $75.00 – 150.00; bottom, (see Engraving chaper for more examples of this scene) wavy California state handle with transfer print of the San Francisco harbor Golden Gate; $100.00 – 150.00.

Plate 793: Top: oranges handle with transfer print oranges in bowl from St. Augustine, Fla.; perfect, $75.00 – 150.00, as is, $20.00 – 30.00; middle: Missouri state handle with transfer print of Eads Bridge, St. Louis; if perfect, $75.00 – 125.00, as is, $20.00 – 30.00; bottom: pattern handle with transfer print of a lumber raft, Duluth, Minnesota; $75.00 – 150.00.

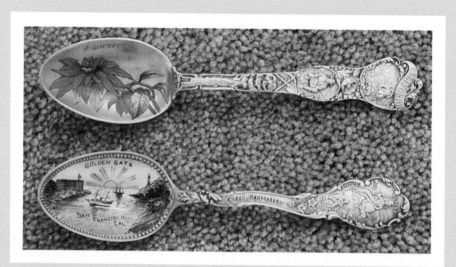

Plate 792

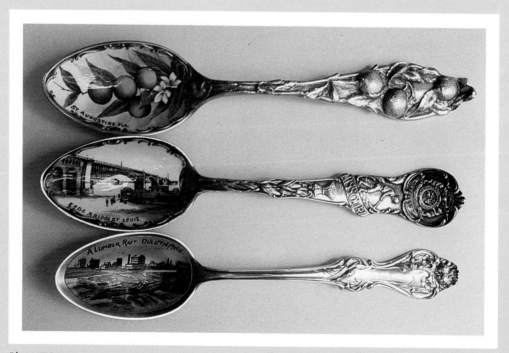

Plate 793

Plate 794: Left: transfer print, Michigan finial above bare breasted, partially draped stylized Art Nouveau lady with "Detroit" engraved in the bowl; $50.00 – 85.00; middle: transfer print, Pennsylvania finial above bare breasted, partially draped stylized Art Nouveau lady with a Carnegie Library embossed bowl; $75.00 – 125.00; right: transfer print, California finial above bare breasted, partially draped stylized Art Nouveau lady with a poorly engraved mission picture in bowl; $50.00 – 70.00.

Plate 795: Left: transfer print, Missouri finial above bare breasted, partially draped stylized Art Nouveau lady with a Joplin, Missouri, mining scene engraved bowl; $100.00 – 175.00; right: transfer print, Arizona finial above bare breasted, partially draped stylized Art Nouveau lady with a poorly engraved punch bowl picture; $50.00 – 85.00.

Plate 794

Plate 795

Plate 796: Top: California state handle with painted yellow flowers, from Pasadena, $100.00 – 175.00; bottom: California state handle with painted red and green poinsettias, from Los Angeles; $100.00 – 175.00.

Plate 797: Top: California state handle with painted picture of the San Gabriel Mission; if perfect, $100.00 – 150.00, as is, $20.00 – 40.00; bottom: multi-scene California state handle with transfer print of the San Francisco Dolores Mission; $100.00 – 175.00.

Plate 796

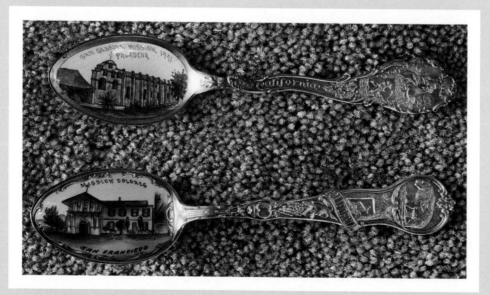

Plate 797

Plate 798: Close-up of Phoenix, Ariz.; State Capitol.

Plate 799: Close-up of transfer print of St. Louis, Mo., City Hall.

Plate 800: Top: Shepard, Missouri wavy handle with transfer print of the St. Louis City Hall; $100.00 – 175.00; bottom: multi-scene, Arizona state handle with transfer print of the Phoenix State Capitol. If perfect, $100.00 – 150.00; as is, $40.00 – 60.00.

Plate 798

Plate 799

Plate 800

Plate 801: Top: Shepard, Kentucky wavy handle state spoon with painted "Pride of Kentucky" horse bowl; $200.00 – 400.00; middle: Shepard, Tennessee wavy handle state spoon with transfer print of a wagon load of cotton bowl; $100.00 – 150.00; bottom: Texas state handle with painted matador and bull scene; $100.00 – 175.00.

Plate 802: Close-up of transfer print of a daily scene in the south showing a wagon load of cotton.

Plate 801

Plate 802

Plate 803: Close-up transfer print of Varied Industries Building from the St. Louis World's Fair; if perfect, $150.00 – 250.00, as is, $30.00 – 55.00.

Plate 804: Top: crossed rifles with Indian and bronco rider finial handle, transfer print picture of a stagecoach "out of the plains;" perfect, $250.00 – 450.00, as is, $100.00 – 125.00; bottom: multi-scene, Iowa state handle with enameled bowl showing corn and rabbits from Cedar Rapids; $50.00 – 75.00.

Plate 803

Plate 804

Plate 805: From top: multi-scene handle, smiling black woman bowl, $250.00 – 400.00; pattern handle with black man eating watermelon, labeled "the real thing;" $300.00 – 450.00; black finial with enameled flower handle and painted watermelon bowl; $250.00 – 400.00; multi-scene handle with black boy holding watermelon slice, $200.00 – 275.00; multi-scene handle with black boy sitting on cotton bale and eating watermelon; $200.00 – 300.00; pattern handle with three black portraits in bowl; $300.00 – 500.00.

Plate 805

Plate 806: From left: multi-scene handle with painted "strange-looking" man riding a burro, and labeled "Galveston, Texas;" $100.00 – 150.00; Florida state handle with transfer print of St. Augustine City Gates bowl; $75.00 – 125.00; flowered Washington state handle with painted picture of a redwood tree which has an opening large enough for a person to walk through; $125.00 – 175.00; flowered handle with transfer print picture of a large woman and smaller people and labeled "It's a shame to take the money." This is probably a satire on some political event; $100.00 – 175.00; Washington state handle with transfer print of "Spokane Falls;" $75.00 – 150.00; simulated tree handle with enameled coat of arms in bowl; $60.00 – 100.00.

Plate 806

Plate 807: From left: embossed San Francisco Golden Gate harbor scene with California orange finial; plain bowl with ostrich (ostrich farms were popular tourist attractions); engraved "Grand Canyon" bowl with painted Indian finial; engraved Santa Barbara, Calif., mission scene with painted oranges finial; engraved "virgin of Cobre" scene with painted pineapple finial; engraved initials in bowl with painted blue flower finial; $50.00 – 125.00 each.

Plate 807

Plate 808: Top: transfer print Illinois finial above bare breasted partially draped stylized Art Nouveau lady with embossed Peoria Courthouse and soldier monument bowl; $75.00 – 150.00; bottom: transfer print finial with plants and ship above bare breasted partially draped stylized Art Nouveau lady with impressed Lookout Mountain, Chattanooga, Tennessee bowl; $75.00 – 150.00.

Plate 809: From left: enameled Oklahoma commemorative on becoming the newest state; Shiebler; $50.00 – 95.00; enameled suits of cards, engraved "W" bowl; Paye and Baker; $45.00 – 85.00; very unusual enameled applied finial showing a Roman soldier stepping on a conquered foe: Latin inscription, "sic semper tyrannis," (from Virginia state seal); Durgin for Greenleaf and Crosby; $30.00 – 75.00; champlevé enameled Duluth, Minnesota, plain bowl; no manuf. mark; $20.00 – 40.00 (detail Plate 776); modern enameled Christmas spoon; Gorham; 1974; $15.00 – 35.00.

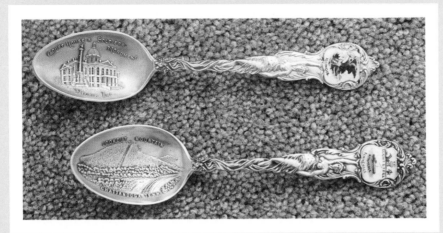

Plate 808

Plate 809

329

The Spoon Club

Spoon collectors have organized several clubs in different parts of the country. These clubs are not for profit and are run by the collectors for their own benefit. New members are always warmly welcomed. There is usually a very small annual membership fee which covers the cost of the newsletter. Some of these clubs also sponsor local spoon or silver shows once a year. There is usually a national convention once each year. The addresses of the clubs are subject to change at any time, but the clubs from different areas are usually in contact with each other. If you do not get a response from the club closest to you, contact the other clubs and they should be able to provide more current addresses or phone numbers. It is quite enjoyable to meet other collectors to swap stories or spoons and to show off your latest "treasure." Most long-term spooners are very friendly and knowledgeable and are happy to talk to new collectors.

Spoon Collectors of Southern California (SCSC)
3832 Denwood Ave.
Los Alamitos, California 90720

Southeastern States Spoon Society (SSSS)
1118 Live Oak St.
New Smyrna Beach, Florida 32168

Northeastern Spoon Collectors Guild
c/o NSCG
P.O. Box 12072
Albany, New York 12212

Dallas Spooners
9748 Broken Bow Rd.
Dallas, Texas 75238

Northwest Spoon Collectors
2387 S. East Camano Dr.
Camano Island, Washington 98292

Daytime Spoon Club of British Columbia
Box 71015
120th Street
Delta, British Columbia, Canada V4C 8E7

There are no regularly published periodicals (except newsletters) devoted exclusively to spoons, but articles about spoons are frequently found in magazines devoted to various antiques or hobbies. The author of these articles can often direct new collectors to established spoon clubs.

Silver Magazine is the only regularly published periodical specializing in silver. It regularly carries articles about spoons. Their address is *Silver Magazine*, P.O. Box 9690, Rancho Santa Fe, California 92067, (619) 756-1054.

Bibliography

Adair, John: *Navajo and Pueblo Silversmiths*, 5th Edition. University of Oklahoma Press: Norman, Oklahoma, 1958

Andren, Erik. *Swedish Silver.* Gramercy Publishing Co,: New York, 1950.

Avery, S.P. *Collection of Spoons.* 1899.

Banister, Judith. *English Silver.* Paul Hamlyn: London, 1969.

Banister, Judith. *English Silver Hallmarks.* 1983.

Bernier, Georges. *The Selective Eye.* Random House: New York, 1955.

Bly, John. *Miller's Silver Marks & Sheffield Plate.* Reed International Books, Ltd.: Great Britain, 1993.

Bowles, Janet and Barry Shifman. *Arts & Crafts Metalwork.* Indianapolis Museum of Art: Indiana, 1993.

Boylan, Leona Davis. *Spanish Colonial Silver.* Museum of New Mexico Press: Santa Fe, New Mexico, 1974.

Burke James H. *American Silver & Silver-Plated Holloware.* Warner Books, Inc.: New York, 1982. General guide, no spoons.

Came, Richard. *Silver.* Octopus Books, Ltd.: London, 1961.

Cederwall, Sandraline. *Spratling Silver.* Chronicle Books: San Francisco, 1990.

Choate, Sharr. *Creative Gold and Silversmithing.* Crown Publishers Inc.: New York, 1970.

Christie 7/87.

Christie 1/89. Wagstaff Collection.

Clayton, Michael. *Collector's Dictionary of Silver & Gold of Great Britain & America.* World Publishing Co.: New York, 1971.

Culme, John/John Strang. *Antique Silver & Silver Collecting.* Hamlyn Publishing Group Ltd.: London, 1973.

Delieb, Eric. *Investing in Silver.* Clarkson N. Potter, Inc.: New York, 1967.

Delieb, Eric. *Silver Boxes.* Exeter Books: New York, 1979.

Divas, Jan. *Gold Marks of the World.* Aventinum: Prague, 1994.

Divas, Jan. *Silver Marks of the World.* Hamlyn, London, 1977.

Dolan, Maryanne. *American Sterling Silver Flatware – Identification Guide.* Books Americana: Florence, Alabama 35630, 1993.

Fales, Martha Gandy. *Early American Silver.* E.P. Dutton & Co.: New York, 1973.

Feild, Rachae. *Buying Antique Silver.* Macdonald & Co., Ltd.: London, 1968.

Fletcher, Lucinda. *Silver.* Crescent Books: New York, 1973.

Georg Jensen Silversmithy. *Renwick Gallery.* Renwick Gallery of the National Arts: Washington D.C., 1980

Glanville, Philippa. *Silver History and Design.* Harry N. Abrams, Inc.: New York, 1996.

Gottschalk, Lillian. *Napkin Rings.* Collector Books: Paducah, Kentucky.

Grimwade, Mark. *Introduction to Precious Metals.* 1985.

Gruber, Alain. *Silverware.* Rizoli International Publications, Inc.: New York, 1982.

Guptill, Arthur L. *Norman Rockwell Illustrator.* Watson-Guptill Publications: New York, 1970.

Hagan, Tere. *Silver-Plated Flatware – Identification Guide.* Collector Books: Paducah, Kentucky, 1981.

Hardt, Anton. *Adventuring Further in Souvenir Spoons.* Greenwich Press: New York, 1971.

Hardt, Anton. *Souvenir Spoons of the 90's.* Greenwich Press: New York, 1972.

Harmsen, Bill. *Sculpture in Silver.* Harmsen Publishing Co.: Denver, 1992.

Helliwell, Stephen. *Small Silver Tableware.* Christie's Bullfinch Press Book: Boston, 1996.

Hind, Arthur M. *History of Engraving and Etching.* Dover Publications, Inc.: New York, 1963.

Hinman, C.W. *Press Working of Metals.* McGraw-Hill Book Co.: New York, 1950.

Holland, Margaret. *English Provincial Silver.* Arco Publishing Co. Inc.: New York, 1971.

Holland, Margaret. *Silver.* Peerage Books: London.

Hood, Graham. *American Silver – A History of Style.* Praeger Publishers: New York, 1971.

Houart, Victor. *L'Argenterie Miniature.* Office du Livre, Fribourg: Switzerland, 1981.

Hughes, G. Bernard. *Small Antique Silverware.* Bramhall House: New York, 1957.

Hughes, Bernard & Therle. *Three Centuries of English Domestic Silver.* Frederick A. Praeger: New York, 1968.

Kauffman, Henry J. *The Colonial Silversmith.* Galahad Books: New York, 1969.

Kolter, Jane. *Early American Silver & Its Makers.* Mayflower Books, Inc.: New York, 1979.

Kovel, Ralph & Terry. *American Silver Marks.* Crown Publishers, Inc.: New York, 1989.

Krekel-Aalberse, Annelies. *Art Nouveau and Art Deco Silver.* Harry N. Abrams, Inc.: New York, 1989.

le Corbeiller, Clare. *European & American Snuff Boxes.* Viking Press: New York, 1966.

Lewis & Morgan. *American Victorian Architecture.* Dover Publications Inc.: New York, 1975.

McGlothlin, Chris A. *World's Fair Spoons, Vol. 1.* Florida Rare Coin Galleries, Inc.: Tallahassee, Florida 1985.

McNab, Jessie. *Silver.* Smithsonian Institution: Washington D.C.,1981.

Moore, Simon. *Spoons 1650 – 1930.* 1987.

Morse, Edgar. *Silver in the Golden State.* Oakland Museum History Department: Oakland, 1986.

Newman, Harold. *Illustrated Dictionary of Silverware.* Thames and Hudson Ltd.: London, 1987.

Osterberg, Richard. *Sterling Silver Flatware.* Schiffer Publishing Ltd.: Atglen, Pennsylvania, 1994.

Pack, Robert. *Collectors Guide to Canadian Souvenir Spoons.* Argentum Cochlear Publishing: Vancouver, Canada, 1995.

Pickford, Ian. *Silver Flatware,* England, Ireland, Scotland 1660+. Antique Collectors Club, Ltd.: Suffolk, Great Britain, 1993.

Rainwater, Dorothy. *American Spoons*. Thomas Nelson & Sons: Camden, New Jersey, 1968.

Rainwater, Dorothy. *Encyclopedia of American Silver Manufacturers*. Schiffer Publishing Co.: West Chester, Pennsylvania,1986.

Rainwater, Dorothy. *Spoons from Around the World*. Schiffer Publishing, Ltd.: Atglen, Pennsylvania, 1992.

Rogozen Treasure. *Bulgarian Academy of Science*. Bulgarian Academy of Science: Sofia, Bulgaria 1989.

Schroeder, Timothy R. *Art of the European Goldsmith*. American Federation of the Arts: New York, 1983.

Semon, Kurt: *Treasury of Old Silver*. Robert M. McBride & Co.: New York, 1947.

Sotheby 1/89

Sotheby 11/89

Sotheby 4/90

Sotheby 10/90

Speltz, Alexander. *The Styles of Ornament*. Dover Publications, Inc.: New York.

Sterling Silver. *Silverplate & Souvenir Spoons*. L-W Inc.: Gas City, Indiana, 1990.

Stow, Millicent. *American Silver*. Gramercy Publishing Co.: New York, 1950.

Tardy. *Poincons d'Argent*, 10th Edition. Tardy: Paris.

Taylor, Gerald. *Silver*. 1963.

Untermyer Collection, *Metropolitan Museum of Art*. Nicholas/David Lithographers: New York, 1977.

Untracht, Oppi. *Enameling on Metal*. Chilton Book Company: Philadelphia, 1957.

Venable, Charles L. *Silver in America 1840 – 1940*. Harry N. Abrams, Inc.: New York, 1994.

Verizzo, Ouida. *American Skyline Souvenir Spoons*. Mel Brethauer: Sarasota, Florida, 1978 limited edition.

Walter Drake. *Flatware Pattern Directory*.

Ward, Barbara McLean. *Silver in American Life*. Yale University Art Gallery, 1979.

Wark, Robert. *British Silver in the Huntington Collection*. Huntington Library & Art Gallery: San Marino, California, 1978.

Warren, David B. *Marks of Achievement*. Harry N. Abrams, Inc.: New York, 1987.

Wenham, Edward. *Old Silver*. Spring Books: London, 1964.

Wenham, Edward. *Practical Book of American Silver*. J.B. Lippincott Co.: Philadephia, 1949.

Wissinger, Joanna. *Arts & Crafts – Metalwork and Silver*. Pavilion Books, Ltd.: London, 1994.

Wyler, Seymour. *The Book of Old Silver, New Edition*. Crown Publishers, Inc.: New York.

Index

About the Author

Wayne Bednersh is a graduate of UCLA and has authored several articles on spoons and silver techniques. His interest in silver medallions and antiques eventually led him to souvenir spoon collecting. His desire to preserve and understand the important historical events found engraved on commemorative spoons has culminated in this extensive narrative about silver souvenir spoons and spoon manufacturing techniques.

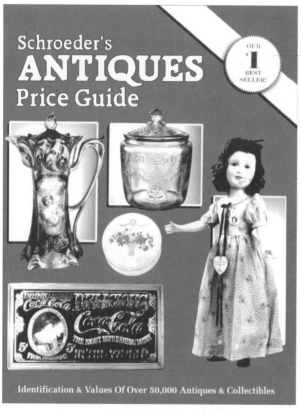